Success guides

Intermediate 1
English

Sheena Greco

Text © 2005 Sheena Greco
Design & layout © 2005 Leckie & Leckie
Cover image © Caleb Rutherford

1st Edition (reprinted 2006)

ISBN 1-84372-284-4
ISBN-13 978-1-84372-284-7

Published by
Leckie & Leckie
3rd Floor
4 Queen Street
Edinburgh
EH2 1JE

Email: enquiries@leckieandleckie.co.uk
Web: www.leckieandleckie.co.uk

Special thanks to
Caleb Rutherford (cover design), Larry Flanagan (content review), Susan Moody (copy-edit), Ken Vail Graphic Design (page make-up), Hamish Sanderson (illustrations), Roda Morrison (proofreading), Fiona Barr (index).

A CIP Catalogue record for this book is available from the British Library.

® Leckie & Leckie is a registered trademark

Leckie & Leckie Ltd is a division of Granada Learning Limited.

Leckie & Leckie has made every effort to trace all copyright holders. If any have been inadvertently overlooked, we will be pleased to make the necessary arrangements.
We would like to thank the following for their permission to reproduce their material:
• Transworld Publishers for extracts from *Down Under* by Bill Bryson (pp 23–26);
• Ian McFadyen for the poem *Scorpions* (p 30);
• John Mannion & Frank Fitzsimons for extracts from *GCSE English and English Literature Success Guide*, published by Letts Educational (pp 41–55);
• Topham Picturepoint for two photographs (pp 46 & 48).

Leckie & Leckie would like to thank the following for permission to reproduce their copyright material without charge:
• The Scottish Qualifications Authority for permission to reproduce past examination questions and extracts from the Intermediate 1 English Arrangements, taken from the SQA website;
• The Random House Group Ltd for extracts from *Round Ireland with a Fridge* by Tony Hawks, published by Ebury Press (pp 17, 20 & 22) and *In Patagonia* by Bruce Chatwin, published by Jonathan Cape (pp 21–22);
• Sarah Roe for an extract from the article 'Ever Been Ad?', taken from *The Scotsman* (pp 22–23);
• Penguin Books Ltd for an extract from *Mary Queen of Scots got her head chopped off* by Liz Lochhead (Penguin Plays, 1989) Copyright © Liz Lochhead, 1989 (p 32);
• Rogers, Coleridge & White Ltd for an extract from the short story 'Getting Sent For' by Agnes Owens, taken from *Lean Tales* (p 34).

Contents

Introduction

Reading

Writing

Personal Study: written

Personal Study: spoken

Assessment

Welcome

Hello and welcome to the *Intermediate 1 English Success Guide*! Being able to communicate in English is a key skill in life and in work. This guide has been written to help you develop this skill and pass the course. Studying English also gives you the chance to **enjoy** reading, writing, talking and listening. So go for it – and have some fun in the process!

In this chapter of the guide, you will find a number of sections.

First, there is an explanation of how the content of the guide is organised, so you will know what to expect right from the start.

The second section gives you some key facts about the Intermediate 1 English course and what it involves.

Finally, the 'Summary' section gives all this information in a series of tables and lists to show you at-a-glance what is involved in the course.

How this guide is organised

The structure of this guide is organised around developing the reading and writing skills you will need to pass all the component parts of the course. So in the **'Reading'** chapter, there is a lot of information about the reading skills you will need to achieve Learning Outcomes in the Language Study (close reading of non-fiction texts) and Literary Study (textual analysis). There is also advice on the reading skills required for your Critical Essay. Likewise, in the **'Writing'** chapter, there is information about the writing skills you will need to achieve the Learning Outcome in the Language Study (Start writing!).

The **'Personal Study'** chapters give useful advice about how to approach this particular unit of the course.

Finally, the **'Assessment'** chapter provides useful information and tips on internal and external assessment and on exam skills in general.

Ask your teacher if you need more advice about the course itself or about any other information in this book. The SQA website is also a very useful source of information (www.sqa.org.uk).

Although the guide is divided into chapters to make it easier to follow, you will probably not work straight through it from start to finish in class – for example, you might work on the skills for Textual Analysis as preparation for your Personal Study.

Intermediate 1 English and what it involves

Here is a brief summary of what is involved in the course and how it is assessed.

The award of Intermediate 1 English is based on a combination of internal and external assessment. What this means is that you have to pass all three **units** or sections of the course, as well as an external examination. The three **units** are as follows:

- Language Study
- Literary Study
- Personal Study

Each of these units has one or more **Learning Outcomes,** or skills, that you will have learned by the end of the course. The **Learning Outcomes** for each **unit** are listed below.

Language Study Unit

Learning Outcome 1

'Understand, analyse and evaluate non-fiction print text which conveys basic information.'

This will require you to read non-fiction passages and then write your answers to a number of questions on the passages.

You can find out more about the reading skills you will need for this Learning Outcome in the **'Reading'** chapter.

Learning Outcome 2

'Compose a piece of writing in a particular genre.'

This will require you to practise extended writing.

You will find out more about the writing skills you will need for this Learning Outcome in the **'Writing'** chapter.

Literary Study Unit

Learning Outcome 1

'Textual analysis of an unseen text.'

This will require you to answer questions on a piece of writing you have not read previously. The text could be either prose or poetry or drama.

You will find out more about the reading skills you will need for this Learning Outcome in the **'Reading'** chapter.

Personal Study Unit

Learning Outcome 1

'Write or speak critically about a chosen text(s) or topic(s).'

This will require you to write or speak about a text(s) or topic(s) showing that you have understood and can analyse and evaluate the text(s) or topic(s).

You will work independently on your Personal Study, although there may be time in class allowed for this.

You will find out more about the skills you will need for this Learning Outcome in the **'Reading'** and **'Personal Study'** chapters.

Internal assessment

The work you do for these Learning Outcomes will be assessed internally. Internal assessments in most schools/colleges are called NABs, because they come from the SQA National Assessment Bank. You may have heard this term around your school/college. In this section of the guide, both terms – internal assessment and NABs – will be used.

External assessment

As well as being assessed internally on the Learning Outcomes for each unit, you also need to sit an external examination, lasting 1 hour and 30 minutes. This has two papers, each lasting 45 minutes:

- Close Reading paper – you have to answer questions on a passage of unseen prose.
- Critical Essay – you answer one question from a range of questions about a text you have previously studied.

At-a-glance summary

Summary of internal and external assessments

Unit	Learning Outcome	Type of assessment
Language Study	LO1 understand, analyse and evaluate non-fiction print text which conveys basic information	internal assessment (NAB) on specified date
	LO2 compose a piece of writing in a particular genre	internal assessment (NAB) on specified date
Literary Study	LO textual analysis of an unseen text	internal assessment (NAB) on specified date
Personal Study	LO write critically about a chosen text(s) or topic(s) or LO speak critically about a chosen text(s) or topic(s)	internal assessment (NAB) on specified date internal assessment (NAB) on specified date
Close Reading	In response to a series of questions, demonstrate ability to understand, analyse and evaluate a passage of unseen prose	external exam
Critical Essay	In response to one question from a range of questions, write a critical essay demonstrating ability to understand, analyse and evaluate previously studied poetry, prose, drama, mass media or language text(s)	external exam

Summary of internal and external course assessments

Internal Assessments (NABs)

- Language Study LO1: Understand, analyse and evaluate non-fiction print text which conveys basic information.
- Language Study LO2: Compose a piece of writing in a particular genre.
- Literary Study LO: Textual analysis of an unseen text.
- Personal Study LO: Write or speak critically about a chosen text(s) or topic(s).

External Assessments

- Close Reading (45 minutes)
- Critical Essay (45 minutes)

Summary of skills for each unit

Language Study	Literary Study	Personal Study	Close Reading	Critical Essay
reading	reading	reading	reading	reading
writing	writing	writing	writing	writing

This table should help you see that the skills you need for each unit are essentially the same. You will probably also know that reading and writing aren't the only skills that you need to pass Intermediate 1 English. Talking and listening are essential to the course – you will discuss many aspects of the texts and topics you study as a way of learning from others. You are **not** assessed formally, however, on talking or listening, unless you present your Personal Study as a talk – more on this in the **'Personal Study: spoken'** chapter.

How much will I need to write?

The following tables show you which units require you to write longer pieces of writing, and which require you to write shorter responses in answer to questions.

Unit	Learning Outcome	Extended writing or questions?	How long?
Language Study	LO1	answer questions	
Language Study	LO2	extended writing	min. 300 words
Literary Study	LO	answer questions	
Personal Study	LO	extended writing speaking	one hour min. 3 mins
Critical Essay	external exam	extended writing	45 mins

Performance criteria/targets: internal assessment

There are a number of performance criteria or targets that you have to meet to achieve the Learning Outcomes in each unit. Here they are.

To achieve LO1 of the Language Study unit, you must:

understand — Show that you can understand the main and less important ideas in the text, and explain how these work together.

analyse — Show that you can explain how the structure, style and language of the text add to the meaning, effect or impact of the text.

evaluate — Show that you can comment on how effective the text is, using evidence, and support this by showing that you know the purpose of the text.

To achieve LO2 of the Language Study unit, you must show that:

content — The content of your writing is appropriate for your audience, and that you have made an attempt to develop a number of ideas.

structure — You have organised your content into an appropriate structure.

expression — You have used appropriate techniques, words, sentence structures and tone.

technical accuracy — Your spelling, punctuation and grammar are mainly accurate.

To achieve LO1 of the Literary Study unit, you must:

understand — Show that you can understand the main and less important ideas in the text, and explain how these work together.

analyse — Show that you can explain how the structure, style and language of the text add to the meaning, effect or impact of the text.

evaluate — Give a personal reaction (can be implied or clearly stated) to the content or style of the text, using references from the text.

To achieve LO1 of the Personal Study, your writing/talk must:

understand — Show that you understand the main points of the subject matter by referring to relevant features of the subject matter.

analyse — Describe some of the more obvious ways in which structure, style and language contribute to meaning, effect and impact.

evaluate — Contain a stated or implied personal reaction to the subject matter, supported by some evidence.

express — Show a clear line of thought and mainly accurate use of spelling, grammar and punctuation.

Performance criteria/targets: external assessment

In your Close Reading, to achieve Intermediate 1 English at Grade C, you must:

understand — Show that you can understand the main and less important ideas in the text, and explain how these work together.

analyse — Show that you can explain how the structure, style and language of the text add to the meaning, effect or impact of the text.

evaluate — Show that you can comment on how effective the text is, using evidence and showing that you know the purpose of the text.

In the Critical Essay, to achieve Intermediate 1 English at Grade C, you must:

understand — Show that you can understand the main ideas in the text by referring to relevant parts of the text.

analyse — Show that you can analyse in simple terms the structure, style and language of the text.

evaluate — Show that you have a personal reaction to the text by referring to relevant parts of the text.

express — Show a clear line of thought and mainly accurate use of spelling, grammar and punctuation.

You will find more information on these performance criteria or targets in the **'Reading'** and **'Writing'** chapters of this guide.

Target Time

If you want to do more than meet the targets at C grade, you will find the 'Target Time' sections helpful. Target Time appears at the end of each chapter in this guide and gives you the chance to reflect on what you have read and to think about the areas you need to work on to achieve the grade you want.

Basic skills

This chapter starts with the basic skills you will need for reading in the Intermediate 1 English course. You may be familiar with some of them already. At any rate, you will need these skills not just for Close Reading and Textual Analysis – you will also use them for your Critical Essay and Personal Study, too.

Skimming

Skimming means reading through information to **get an overall impression** of it. You are not looking for any specific information but just **'getting the gist'** of the text.

Skimming is usually done quite quickly. After skimming, have a go at writing a few short notes on the text, including what you remember about:

- the layout
- what it is about
- one or two of the main points.

Scanning

Scanning is also done quite quickly but this time you are looking for **particular information**. This is a really useful skill to have when you are researching a text or topic for your Personal Study or maybe reading through a Close Reading passage for a specific answer.

When you are scanning, you are looking for **key words** and **phrases**. If you scan successfully, you will have found the **key information** you are looking for. For example, you might be looking for evidence of geographical setting to use in your Critical Essay. The **key words** you would be scanning for, therefore, would be the names of towns and countries, words that describe geographical settings and perhaps words that describe the atmosphere of a particular place.

Highlighting

The humble highlighter is one of the greatest inventions known to man, woman or student! Use yours to highlight **words, phrases** and **ideas** that you want to **remember** or **emphasise**. Use different colours to highlight different ideas. Or if you are writing about the three main characters in a novel, for example, use a different colour for each character.

Highlighters can also be used when you are **scanning** or when you are **reading in great detail**. You might be asked to find **facts** (statements which cannot be argued and are true) or **opinions** (the writer's point of view) or **imaginative detail** (ideas the writer has made up). Again, you could use a different colour for each.

Researching material

Being able to research material is a vital skill, and it is particularly useful in your Personal Study and/or Critical Essay. Your teacher might want you to research certain types of writing for your Language Study unit, too. The internet and books can both be excellent sources of information.

You will find skimming and scanning invaluable when you come to research material – these skills save time and effort when you are trawling through large amounts of information.

Learn how to use search engines effectively – there really is a skill in it. For example, if you type in '**horror stories**', you will find literally thousands of examples – good, bad and indifferent. However, type in '**Dr Jekyll and Mr Hyde by Robert Louis Stevenson**' and hey presto! you've got a specific (and brilliant) example of the genre. The more specific you are, the better.

If you don't have a computer at home, try your local school/college library for access to the internet or to books, encyclopaedias and so on. Technology is brilliant – but so are books. In fact, books can sometimes have more detailed and better quality information than the internet. Don't dismiss them.

As always, your teacher will help you if you are struggling to access appropriate research material.

Note-taking

There are many ways to take notes. Taking notes means **writing down ideas with less detail** than in the original text. You will probably have a method you prefer. Some students, for example, like to take 'linear' notes under headings, using short sentences, dashes and underlining (or of course highlighting!) for emphasis. Others prefer mind-mapping. This involves placing your key idea in the middle of the page, and having your 'sub' ideas grow out of this.

The main point about notes is that they save you from writing everything out 'long-hand'. To take notes effectively, use abbreviations and short phrases and leave out punctuation and unnecessary words.

However, try to make sure your notes make sense. Otherwise at revision time, you won't understand what you have written, and why you thought it was of vital importance at the time!

Also, make sure you organise your notes, or you might lose a page containing a crucial thought or idea! Keeping them in a binder or a notebook with different sections is a good idea.

Summarising

Summarising means **explaining clearly and concisely the key points and ideas of a book, film, article, etc.** For example, when you explain the plot of a film you have seen, you are summarising it.

Summarising is a useful skill in the appropriate context, whether you are writing or talking. You can get over the most important details without sending your reader or listener to sleep!

Close Reading: skills

What is the difference between fiction and non-fiction?

This section of the book is all about non-fiction texts. In non-fiction writing, the writer gives the reader **information** or **opinions** about a subject. For example, a book on the history of Mary, Queen of Scots would be non-fiction. On the other hand, fiction is **imaginative** writing that writers make up 'in their heads' although it can be **based** on real events and real people. An example of fiction would be *Lord of the Rings*. Non-fiction is the opposite of fiction.

The non-fiction texts you read will contain plenty of detail but they will be clear and easy to understand. They will give you information, along with ideas and/or opinions. No problem!

There are three very important terms which we will now look at – purpose, audience and format. You must understand them before reading any text.

Quick Think

Which do you prefer reading – fiction or non-fiction? Why? Can you remember the title of the most recent fiction you read? What about the most recent non-fiction?

Purpose

Purpose means the reason the writer has written a piece of writing. All writers want to give you information and that is often their main purpose. They will have other purposes, too – perhaps to express opinions, persuade, create, reflect or argue.

Pair and Share

Look at the diagram below. It shows how you can write about one topic in different ways for different purposes. There are four different types of writing illustrated here – all related to the same topic – and each has at least two purposes. Get together with your partner and discuss which you think is the main purpose for each type of writing.

Fox hunting: one topic, four different types of writing, two purposes	
1 A letter to a newspaper from a Master of the Hunt – purpose: to inform, to educate	3 A love story about two hunt saboteurs – purpose: to inform, to entertain, to create
2 A paragraph in a Modern Studies textbook – purpose: to inform, to educate	4 A poster for an anti-fur charity – purpose: to inform, to entertain, to shock

Quick Think

Which of the texts in the table above would you prefer to read? Why?

Two-minute Task

Read the extract below and work out what the purpose of the writing is.

It makes my blood boil! Terrified foxes, running in terror from those bloodthirsty hounds! I am aware that foxes have to be culled, but hunting turns fox killing into a game, and that is surely not right!

Audience

Audience simply means the people who read the text. A simple way to understand this term is to think of the audience in a theatre or for a TV programme. Plays, programmes and books are all written with an audience in mind.

Look at the list below and see if you can work out the **main** audience for each. (Keep in mind that there are a lot of adults out there who love children's films and television programmes.)

Text	Audience?
Documentary about retirement	
Book about looking after household pets	
Saturday morning pop music programme	
Theatre adaptation of Roald Dahl's *The Twits*	

Quick Think

If you were writing a book or making a film/TV programme, what audience would you write or make it for? Why?

Format

The third term you must know is **format**. The format of a text is very easy to work out. Is the text written in columns? Is it written in paragraphs? Does it have a headline or heading? Is it set out in a particular 'pattern'?

Look at the following shapes or formats. Can you tell – just by looking at the shapes – what type of text it is?

Well done if you recognised that the first is a letter and the second is a newspaper article.

All three terms – **purpose**, **audience** and **format** – will help you understand a text and will help you to answer the questions on the text as well.

Worked example: Round Ireland with a Fridge by Tony Hawks

Now it is time to look at an example.

Audience and purpose

The first thing to do when you read through a non-fiction text is to work out the **audience** and **purpose**. Read through the passage at least twice **before** you look at the questions. Your first reading is to get a quick overall impression about the text – look at the beginning of this section to remind yourself about **skimming**. As you read the text for the first time, ask the following questions:

What is the purpose of the text?

Which audience is the writer trying to reach?

Pair and Share

Round Ireland with a Fridge

In the passage that follows, the writer and entertainer Tony Hawks describes his first visit to Ireland and the effect it had on him.

Read the first three paragraphs below and work out the purpose and audience. Talk this over with a partner and agree on your decision.

In 1989 I went to Ireland for the first time. I don't know why it had taken so long. Some parts of the world you make a conscious effort to visit and others have to wait until fate delivers you there.

When the moment arrived for me to set foot on the Emerald Isle, it was as a result of a badly written song. An Irish friend from London, Seamus, had urged me to compose a piece for him and his mate Tom to sing at an International Song Competition which was held each year in his home town. Qualification for the final, he explained, was a formality provided I agreed to do a twenty-minute comedy set for the audience whilst the judges were out. Seamus wanted to perform a humorous song, and had asked me to come up with something that would "set it apart" from the other entries. In the event, what would set it apart would be a quite significant drop in standard.

The song I had written was called "I Wanna Have Tea With Batman". Now I consider myself to be a good songwriter, but this song was – how can I put it? – yes, that's it – poor. To their credit, Seamus and Tom conjured up a performance to match it.

Did you think the passage was written for more than one audience? Correct! The audience might be people who enjoy reading about travel or who like humorous writing, children or adults; the general public.

What are the main ideas in the text?

Writers often structure their work so that there is one main idea per paragraph. (This is a good way of structuring your own writing.)

As you read through each paragraph, ask yourself 'What is the main idea in this paragraph?'

Two-minute Task

Read through the text for a second time – it helps you to go into more detail. This time round read more carefully and slowly through the passage, trying to understand the sense of each sentence as you read. What are the main points in this section of the text?

Check out the list below, and see how many of the main points you noticed:

- Author went to Ireland 1989
- Song written for competition
- Seamus and Tom to sing
- Author to do comedy set
- 'Batman' – a bad song
- Bad performance

If you can work out the main ideas on your second reading, you will then have a good understanding of the passage before you even look at the questions. And read the passage for a third or fourth time, if you need to – you won't be able to answer the questions properly until you can understand what the passage is about.

Then again, you may come across words you don't understand during this process. Don't let these put you off! You can usually work out the meaning of an unfamiliar word from its context (the other words and phrases surrounding it). Here is an example.

Two-minute Task

Look for the word 'conscious' in paragraph 1 of the Tony Hawks extract, *Round Ireland with a Fridge*. Imagine for a moment that you do not know what 'conscious' means. Look round about the word 'conscious' for a word that may help in the same sentence. Did you find 'fate'? You know that 'fate' means 'chance' so you can guess that 'conscious' means 'deliberate' or 'thought out'. So the author is telling us that sometimes we visit countries by chance and sometimes we plan to visit them.

Close Reading: questions

Time now to think about the **questions** you will be asked on the Close Reading passage. You will notice in all your practice passages that the questions are always followed by the letter **U** or **A** or **E**. These letters are there to help you:

U stands for **Understanding**

A stands for **Analysis**

E stands for **Evaluation**.

You need to demonstrate that you have all of these three skills if you are to pass the Intermediate 1 English course.

Understanding

'**U**' or **Understanding** questions ask you **what** the passage is about.

Your answers must show that you understand both the main and the less important ideas in the text. In an 'Understanding' question, you are not being asked about **why** the author has used particular words or about your **opinion** of the ideas in the text. 'Understanding' questions simply ask you to explain **what** the writer has said.

Two-minute Task

Look at this '**U**' question on the Tony Hawks extract, *Round Ireland with a Fridge*, on page 17:

In the opening paragraph, the writer gives two different explanations for visiting 'parts of the world'.

In your own words, say what they are. 2 (U)

Have a go at answering this question and remember – the number of marks helps you to work out how much to write.

Let us look at how you got on. This question is asking you to find two reasons, and obviously you would have to work out the meaning of 'conscious', as we did on the previous page!

Also, note that the answer must be in your own words, so you cannot repeat the words 'conscious' or 'fate'.

A good answer would be:

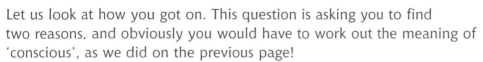

The writer is telling us that sometimes we visit countries by chance and sometimes we plan to visit them.

Two-minute Task

You can never practise enough, so here is another '**U**' question on the Tony Hawks extract, *Round Ireland with a Fridge*, on page 17:

The writer's visit to Ireland was as a result of an invitation to write a song for his friends.

What else did he have to do to ensure they would qualify for the Final of the competition? 2 (U)

Have a go at answering this question and again, remember – the number of marks helps you to work out how much to write.

How did you get on this time? The major clue here is in the second paragraph. Again, remember that the answer must be in your own words so you cannot repeat the words 'comedy set'.

A good answer would be:

He had to entertain the audience during the judging.

Remember! 'U' or Understanding questions ask you **what** the passage is about.

Analysis

'**A**' or **Analysis** questions ask you **why** the writer has written in a particular way.

Analysis questions ask you to **analyse why** the writer has chosen a particular structure, style, word, phrase, image, etc.

Two-minute Task

Look at this '**A**' question on the Tony Hawks extract, *Round Ireland with a Fridge*, on page 17:

By referring to paragraph three, explain how the writer's word-choice and punctuation help to create an informal, conversational tone. 4 (A)

Have a go at answering this question and remember once more that the number of marks will help you work out how much to write.

How did you get on? Did you work out that the writer is addressing the reader directly as though he is having a conversation with you? You could also point out that the dashes indicate he is 'thinking aloud' or pausing as we do in normal conversation. You could write that the question mark followed by an explanation shows he is thinking to himself ...

We know what you're thinking ...

We know that candidates find Analysis questions the hardest in Close Reading, so we shall spend some more time on this. Let us look at each aspect of style that you might be asked about, using an example from a past or specimen Intermediate 1 Close Reading paper.

Tone

Just as you can speak in a certain tone of voice, a writer can write in a certain tone. If you find this concept difficult, try reading the text aloud – in your head! A writer can be sarcastic, affectionate, arrogant, funny – the list is endless. Work out the tone from the words used and always remember to quote the words or phrases in your answer.

Read the following paragraph from *In Patagonia* by Bruce Chatwin – a famous travel writer – in which he describes how a former ship's captain sends a dead animal to London.

> Directly he saw the brontosaurus poking out of the ice, he knew what to do. He had it jointed, salted, packed in barrels and shipped to the Natural History Museum in South Kensington. I pictured blood and ice, flesh and salt, gangs of workmen and lines of barrels along a shore – a work of giants and all to no purpose: the brontosaurus went rotten on its voyage through the tropics and arrived in London a putrefied mess: which was why you saw brontosaurus bones in the museum, but no skin.

Which of these words best describes this paragraph:

- sad?
- comic (funny)?
- ironic?

You could actually choose any of the words above. It is sad **and** ironic because the captain obviously spent quite some time preparing the animal – 'jointed, salted, packed' – only for it to become a useless 'putrefied mess'. The tone is also comic – 'which was why you saw bones in the museum, but no skin'.

Sentence structure

Sentences can be short, long, complex or simple – but they always have a shape.

Complex sentences have a complicated shape and lots of **clauses** or **phrases**, sometimes divided by **commas**. Here is an example:

> I pictured blood and ice, flesh and salt, gangs of workmen and lines of barrels along a shore – a work of giants and all to no purpose: the brontosaurus went rotten on its voyage through the tropics and arrived in London a putrefied mess: which was why you saw brontosaurus bones in the museum, but no skin.

Simple sentences have few phrases and a simple shape.

Here is an example:

> The cat sat on the mat.

Writers choose patterns or shapes for their sentences deliberately. For example, a writer usually places a word in an unusual position to emphasise it. Then again, a writer may use a very long sentence with a long list of verbs to emphasise a lot of action, or may use a very short sentence to draw attention to a word.

Look at the first sentence from the passage by Bruce Chatwin on page 21. Why do you think the writer has written:

Directly he saw the brontosaurus poking out of the ice ...

Instead of:

He saw the brontosaurus poking out of the ice directly ... ?

Here is another example of use of sentence structure from the 2004 Close Reading passage about Tony Hawks visiting Ireland. Later in the passage, he writes about Seamus:

One had to admire his courage, for he was performing in front of his home town and everyone he had grown up with was there: friends, family, teachers, priests, shopkeepers, barmen, drunks – all were rooting for him.

A question was asked about sentence structure:

The writer feels that one 'had to admire' Seamus's courage.
Explain how one feature of the sentence structure helps to convey this feeling. 2 (A)

In the answer, you are expected to point out that the sentence contains a list of examples – emphasising all the different people in the audience – or that the dash or word order emphasises the word 'all' to show how many people were there.

Formal/informal language

It is important to be able to tell the difference between formal and informal language. Not only must you be able to know this when you are reading but you must also be aware of the difference in your own writing.

Informal (sometimes called 'colloquial') language is the sort of everyday language that you use when you are talking or writing to friends or family. On the other hand, you use formal language when you are applying for a job, writing an exam paper or making a presentation.

Here are some of the characteristics of each.

Formal	Informal
no slang	slang
no abbreviations	abbreviations (isn't instead of 'is not')
complex sentences	simple sentences
complex words	simple words

Here is an example.

In 2002, the Close Reading passage was part of a newspaper article about sandwich boards as a form of advertising – these are boards which people carry or hold up around town.

It has to be one of the oldest and most primitive forms of advertising, but even in the hi-tech world of the 21st century, flesh and blood human signposts still turn heads.

Candidates were asked to write down a formal expression from later in the passage which meant the same as 'human signposts still turn heads'. There were three to choose from:

Whether it is amusement, curiosity or sympathy that <u>attracts attention</u>, companies say that when it comes to promoting a product, <u>the human factor works</u> ...

... a living breathing advert <u>that attracts more attention</u> than a two week billboard ...

Narrative stance

You already know that the narrator is the writer – the person 'telling the story'. Writers or narrators **always** have an attitude towards what they are writing. For example, writers who hate football hooliganism will make this very clear through their choice of words. Or they may want you to sympathise with a character, or be trying to persuade you to buy a product. The writer's **stance** is clear through the choice of topic and the words used.

Here is an example.

In 2003, the exam passage was adapted from a book by the famous travel writer, Bill Bryson, in which he described his experiences of boogie-boarding (similar to surfing) in Australia.

Candidates were asked several questions about the writer's stance – in other words, about Bill Bryson's feelings towards boogie-boarding.

Sighing, I shuffled into the pale green and cream-flecked water. The bay was surprisingly shallow. We trudged perhaps 100 feet out and it was still only a little over our knees ...

What word choice shows that the writer was not keen to try boogie-boarding?

Did you pick out 'sighing' or 'shuffled' or 'trudged'? Well done! These words show his reluctance to go into the water and his mood.

Imagery

Writers use images to help us visualise ideas. They can use **metaphors** (her eyes sparkled like diamonds) and **similes** (as alike as peas in a pod) to do this. Metaphors and similes describe things in unusual ways. For example, 'the car purred quietly through the night' (car takes on the characteristics of a cat), or, 'cars stretched like a ribbon along the main street' (the cars are compared to a ribbon).

An image which describes an object as though it is a living thing is called a 'personification'. For example, 'His trainer soles hissed on the linoleum corridors' – the sound of the shoe soles is compared to a snake.

Quick Think

Look out for examples of metaphor, simile and personification in the list below.

The oil rig nodded at me like some prehistoric animal.
As soft as velvet, the leopard's fur shone in the African sun.
'You are a little monkey', snapped Sylvia's mother.
Looking down from the helicopter, the landscape spread out like a giant chess board.
Garth was hissing words like spitting sparks from a fire.

Two-minute Task

Writers of all genres use imagery. A newspaper article or a poem or an advert can all contain word imagery. Look at the poem below. Can you find any similes in the poem? Talk this over with a partner and come to a decision.

A Red Red Rose

Oh my luve is like a red, red rose
That's newly sprung in June:
Oh my luve is like a melodie,
That's sweetly play'd in tune.

As fair art thou, my bonnie lass,
So deep in luve am I:
And I will luve thee still, my dear,
Till a' the seas gang dry.

Till a' the seas gang dry, my dear,
And the rocks melt wi' the sun:
And I will luve thee still, my dear,
While the sands o' life shall run.

And fare thee weel, my only luve!
And fare thee weel a while!
And I will come again, my luve,
Tho it were ten thousand mile!

Robert Burns

Let us go back again to the 2003 boogie-boarding passage where Bill Bryson describes his friend Glenn taking photographs.

Candidates were asked how attention was drawn to the sound of the camera in the sentence below:

Bizeet, bizeet, bizeet, his camera sang as he took three quick and ingeniously identical photographs of Deirdre and me in conversation.

Did you spot the metaphor 'the camera sang'? You might be asked to comment on how effective an image is as well as recognise it. It may be helpful to remember that the stronger the comparison, the more effective the image.

In the example above, the camera is described as if it is singing. What do you think of this image? Is it effective because the sound of a camera is very similar to singing or do you think a camera's shutter is not usually a pleasant melodious sound and so it is not a very effective metaphor? Remember there is no right or wrong answer if you are asked about the effectiveness of an image. Just explain carefully your opinion.

Punctuation

You may be asked why a writer has used certain punctuation, such as an exclamation mark or brackets or a lot of commas. Remember that writers must write grammatically but they often use punctuation for effect – an exclamation mark can mean a character is shocked or surprised. Brackets may be used to explain something in more detail.

Here is an example.

It was a big U-shaped bay, edged by low scrub hills, with what seemed to me awfully big waves pounding in from a vast and moody sea: in the middle distance, several foolhardy souls in wet-suits were surfing towards some foamy outbursts on the rocky headland; nearer in, a scattering of paddlers were being continually, and it seemed, happily engulfed by explosive waves.

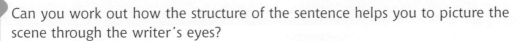

Can you work out how the structure of the sentence helps you to picture the scene through the writer's eyes?

There are three sections to this sentence – look for the semi-colons. They separate each section. The first section is about the bay and its waves, the second is about some surfers and the final section describes some paddlers nearer the shore. So the structure helps you to realise that the writer first describes the whole bay, then the surfers at a distance, then the paddlers who are closer to shore.

Linking words and phrases

Words can be linked together by conjunctions such as 'and', 'but' and 'so'. They can be used at the start of sentences, for example, 'however', 'secondly' and 'later'. They can also link paragraphs together to make the writing flow, for example, 'Although earlier I suggested that man had ruined all known rainforests, there is one example which remains unexplored ...' Here, the phrase 'Although earlier' shows us that the writer is referring back and is also about to start writing about a new topic.

Here is an example.

The exam paper in 2000 contained a newspaper article about how yo-yos are becoming popular again. The writer describes a trip to buy a yo-yo for his son's birthday in the first part of the passage – this description of the shopping trip is then followed by a description of how he eventually becomes annoyed with the boy playing with the yo-yo!

The second section starts with 'Two days later ...' and candidates were asked:

In what ways does the writer link the paragraph beginning 'Two days later ...' to what has gone before?

This phrase is called a **time linking phrase** – the phrase refers back to the mention in the first section of the birthday shopping trip.

Word choice

A writer chooses words very carefully and deliberately, because of the associations they have. 'Drizzle feathers his face' – in this sentence, the writer has chosen the words 'drizzle' and 'feathers' carefully to describe the rain and how it is touching the character's face. You will always be asked about the words the writer has chosen.

In 'Boogie-Boarding', the writer is scared about trying out the sport. Look at the following phrases from the passage. Can you spot which words or phrases show his feelings about boogie-boarding?

'What about sharks?', I asked uneasily

'... we began to strip down – slowly and deliberately in my case, eager in hers – ...'

'I would surface, gasping and confused ...'

'I was resigned to my fate and knew that eventually it would be over.'

There is further advice on these aspects of style in the section on Textual Analysis.

Finally – remember! 'A' or Analysis questions ask you **why** the writer has written in a particular way.

Evaluation

'E' or **Evaluation** questions ask for your **opinion**.

To answer Evaluation questions, you have to express your opinions about the passage.

Evaluation questions ask you to comment on the **ideas** and **words** in the passage.

They often ask, for example, how effective an idea or image or word is. In other words, you are being asked to judge whether an idea or image or word 'fits' in the passage and why. Make sure you get plenty of practise at answering Evaluation questions and remember – you **must** know the author's **purpose** before you can even start to answer them. **'E'** questions ask you **how well** the writer has achieved his or her purpose.

Two-minute Task

Here is an Evaluation question on the Bill Bryson passage.

I positioned myself for the first wave, jumped aboard and sank like an anvil.

Comment on the effectiveness of the humour in this sentence. 2 (E)

Have a go at answering this question and remember – the number of marks is a guide to how much to write.

How did you get on? Remember, you are being asked your opinion about the writer's skill. What do you think of this image? Is it appropriate? If so, you need to explain why.

Two good answers would be:

It is effective because the first part of the sentence is positive and hopeful followed by the writer's sudden sinking.

It is effective because the simile 'sank like an anvil' shows how heavily and suddenly he sank.

Whatever your answer is, you must show that you have a personal opinion about its effect.

You can also be asked to evaluate a whole passage or part of a passage – not just one or two sentences. An Evaluation question from *In Patagonia* (on page 21) asked you whether, after reading the passage, you thought the writer had been successful in describing his childhood experience. Don't give your **own** opinions about your childhood and explain how you found an interesting fossil once! You are evaluating how well the writer has described **his** experience by using evidence from the passage.

And that's all there is to it. Your teacher will give you plenty of practice in answering questions on non-fiction passages. The questions will aways be marked with a '**U**', '**A**' or '**E**' to help you.

Quick Think

Understanding

Analysis

Evaluation

Check back if you are still not clear about the difference between these three types of question. Summarise what each involves, so it is clear in your head.

All your answers should be written in sentences, and it helps if these make sense! They should be in your own words unless you are actually asked to **quote** or **find evidence** from the text.

Remember that Close Reading is part of your external examination in Intermediate 1 English, so it is crucial that you practise answering questions within a given time. There is advice on this in the **'Assessment'** chapter.

Target Time

To achieve Intermediate 1 English at Grade C in your Close Reading, you must give evidence of the following:

Understanding Show that you can understand the main and less important ideas in the text and explain how these work together.

Analysis Show that you can explain how the structure, style and language of the text add to the meaning, effect or impact of the text.

Evaluation Show that you can comment on how successful the text is, using evidence and showing that you know the purpose of the text.

To gain a Grade A, you have to do more ...

Understanding Show that you have a **secure** understanding of the main and less important ideas in the text and explain how these work together **in detail.**

Analysis Show that you can explain **in detail** how the structure, style and language of the text add to the meaning, effect or impact of the text.

Evaluation Show that you can comment on how effective the text is, using **detailed** evidence, **critical terminology** and showing that you know the purpose of the text and the **writer's stance**.

Time to set **your** targets for your Close Reading. Refer back to pages 9 and 10 for more information on target setting.

My target is to achieve Grade .... in my Close Reading because

....

....

....

To achieve this grade, I am going to work on

....

....

....

Textual Analysis

What is textual analysis?

Textual Analysis is when you answer questions on a **fiction** text. The questions asked are very similar to those asked on non-fiction and you will apply many of the same approaches and skills that you used when working through Close Reading non-fiction passages. The skills you need for Textual Analysis are also the same as those for Close Reading:

- Understanding
- Analysis
- Evaluation

So it is all very familiar!

In this section of the book, we will look at examples of a **poem**, an extract from a **play** and a **prose** extract – all from past Intermediate 1 English assessments. Remember that in your assessment, your text may come from any of these three genres. In class, you will study examples from at least two of these genres as well as from (possibly) mass media. This might include a film or an extract from an article in a magazine. You will then have a formal assessment on a specified date.

The Textual Analysis passages you will read will include Scottish texts – the examples here are all by Scottish writers.

Poetry

Worked example:
Scorpions by Ian McFadyen

The best way to understand a poem is simply to read it through and think about it – enjoy it and reflect on it. Hopefully, there will be time for you to do this in your English course. One of the best ways of looking at a poem in more detail to answer questions about it, is to place it in the middle of a page and 'take notes' round it. Underline words, circle images, put question marks beside words and images and write notes at the edge. Develop your own way of doing this – it will help you to answer the questions.

Look at the example below – the notes, underlinings and so on will help you work out the meaning of the poem.

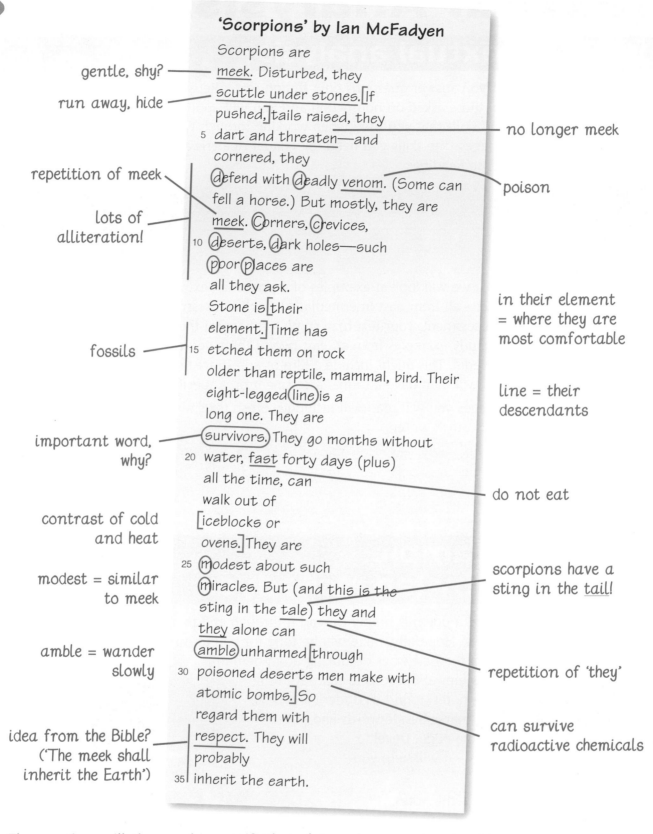

'Scorpions' by Ian McFadyen

Scorpions are
meek. Disturbed, they — gentle, shy?
scuttle under stones. [If — run away, hide
pushed,] tails raised, they
5 dart and threaten—and — no longer meek
cornered, they
defend with deadly venom. (Some can — poison
fell a horse.) But mostly, they are — repetition of meek
meek. Corners, crevices, — lots of alliteration!
10 deserts, dark holes—such
poor places are
all they ask.
Stone is [their
element.] Time has — in their element = where they are most comfortable
15 etched them on rock — fossils
older than reptile, mammal, bird. Their
eight-legged line is a — line = their descendants
long one. They are
survivors. They go months without — important word, why?
20 water, fast forty days (plus) — do not eat
all the time, can
walk out of
[iceblocks or — contrast of cold and heat
ovens.] They are
25 modest about such — modest = similar to meek
miracles. But (and this is the — scorpions have a sting in the tail!
sting in the tale) they and
they alone can — repetition of 'they'
amble unharmed [through — amble = wander slowly
30 poisoned deserts men make with
atomic bombs.] So — can survive radioactive chemicals
regard them with
respect. They will — idea from the Bible? ('The meek shall inherit the Earth')
probably
35 inherit the earth.

The questions will always ask you to find, explain and comment on key ideas – this poem is all about the behaviour and features and nature of the scorpion so it is no surprise that you will be asked questions about these!

Of course, poetry questions will always ask about **structure** or **layout** – the pattern or 'look' of the poem on the page. Does the poem **rhyme**, what is the **rhythm** (handy hint – read the poem quietly but aloud several times to work this out) and does it have **verses**? Are some lines more important than others? Why are words placed in particular positions?

You will always be asked how a writer creates **mood** and their **creation** of a sense of **place**. Another handy hint is that this is usually done through description involving the five senses – sight, sound, smell, touch and taste.

You will be asked many questions about word choice – these are the poet's basic tools, after all. The associations of a word are very important for a poet – why does the poet choose to use 'meek' or 'deadly' or 'amble'? You must know not only what the words mean but also why they have been used.

Quick Think

Which is the main sense used in this poem? Did you realise that it is a very visual poem and that the poet takes care to help you 'see' the scorpion? Can you quote some words from the poem that describe in a visual way what the scorpion looks like and how it moves, where it lives and how it behaves?

A poet can use all or any of the techniques below. Your teacher will tell you more about these.

- imagery
- rhyme
- onomatopoeia

- structure
- word choice
- repetition

- rhythm
- alliteration
- word order

Two-minute Task

This poem makes sense if you write it out in prose. Try that now – write the poem out in normal sentences. This will help you to understand that the poet has made deliberate choices about where to place words and lines. Why not do this and then explain why you think he has placed 'meek' at the start of the second line or 'survivors' at the beginning of a line?

Drama

Worked example: *Mary Queen of Scots got her head chopped off* by Liz Lochhead

Have a read through of this scene from a play first performed in 1987. The crucial thing to remember is that, when we are reading drama, the characters tell us directly what we need to know! We learn about the characters through what they themselves say or do or through what other characters say or do to them. This is called 'characterisation'.

You will be asked about the feelings and emotions of the characters as well as more obvious things like who is speaking to whom. Remember that the words have been chosen deliberately by the playwright to create a particular effect. Note the way the extract is set out with the characters' names at the side. As you read, try to 'picture' the characters and 'hear' the different voices of each in your head.

Reading

In this scene, Mary Queen of Scots is nursing her husband, Darnley, who has the measles.

Darnley in bed, Mary by his bedside

Darnley	Your majesty, is it you?
Mary	Yes, it's me. It's Mary.
Darnley	This is humiliating.
Mary	Wheesht!
Darnley	Measles! A childhood complaint, it's –
Mary	I had it in France when I was a wee wee girl!
Darnley	You poor little thing, so far away from your mother too.
Mary	Aye. I grat full sore for her!
Darnley	I don't know how she could have sent you away. You must have been such a pretty child.
Mary	I dinna ken 'boot that. But I missed her. (*Pause.*) She had to dae it though to keep me safe an' soond. There were plenty plots to steal the infant Queen and rule in her stead. (*Pause.*) If I had a child though … I dinna think I could send ma ain bairn awa'.
Darnley	Poor Mary!
Mary	Oot on the deck, ready tae embark, an 'Ah wis sae excitit – I'm a great sailor, ye ken, I wis the only wan no seeck a' the wey tae France – but, ma mither, she wis greetin' an' roarin' and stitchin' wee medals o' the Blessed Virgin intae ma claes tae keep me safe, I didna ken whit was the maitter, I didna realize hoo lang it'd be e'er I'd see her again.
Darnley	My mother's a Catholic, too!
Mary	Is she?
Darnley	Oh, yes. I can't imagine my mother ever sending me away!
Mary	No' even for your ain guid?
Darnley	I don't think so! (*Laughing*) I'm glad she's not here now, she'd be rushing around with junkets and milk jellies and broth to get my strength back up!
Mary	I brocht you some broth! I forgot! That wis why I came! It'll be cauld noo, I'll go get some mair.
Darnley	Mary, don't – I'm not hungry!
Mary	Do ye not want onything?
Darnley	No. Just … stay with me, Mary.

First, some straightforward Understanding tasks.

What is unusual about how Darnley first addresses Mary? Do you think a husband would normally address as wife as 'Your majesty'?

Why is Darnley embarrassed about having the measles – did you spot the phrase 'A childhood complaint'? He is obviously embarrassed about having an illness usually caught by a young child!

Why does Mary's mother send her away to France? Well done if you thought that this was because her mother felt Mary would be safer abroad.

Pair and Share

You will have noticed that Mary speaks with a strong Scottish accent, using Scottish vocabulary such as 'wheesht' and 'cauld'. What do you think of how she speaks – is it surprising and why? The way she speaks contrasts with how Darnley speaks – again, is this effective and why?

Talk this over with a partner and agree on your decision.

Pair and Share

Which character is which? Can you match up these descriptions and quotations with the correct character?

Talk this over with a partner and agree on your decision.

Character	Personality	Evidence
Mary's mother		'She had to dae it ...'
Darnley's mother	caring	
Darnley	sympathetic	
Mary		'But I missed her.'

In the play, Darnley is portrayed as a childish, arrogant man. Is there any evidence here which backs up either of these descriptions? What do you think of the character of Mary? Look at her description of her journey to France – would you agree that she had to 'grow up' quickly given her situation?

Remember to read the stage directions. They are written by the playwright to tell us about what the characters do and how they do it, for example, how to enter the stage or how to make a movement. The stage directions are in italics.

Two-minute Task

Look at the stage directions for Mary – there are two pauses as she is describing her childhood. If you were the director, how would you tell the actor playing Mary how to act and speak during these lines?

Think about what the pauses might be for. Crying? Hesitating? Perhaps to show she cannot remember?

Practise for a drama Textual Analysis by watching and reading plays – as many as you can and as often as you can!

Prose

Worked example: *The Lighthouse* by Agnes Owens

Most pupils prefer to answer questions on a prose passage in Textual Analysis. Whichever genre you prefer, the best way to improve your Textual Analysis skills is to read as many examples as you can of the genre. Your teacher will advise you about what to read.

Look at the following list of techniques:

- tone
- imagery
- narrative stance
- punctuation
- sentence structure
- word choice
- linking

These should all sound familiar. If they don't, look back at the Close Reading section and you will find examples of all these techniques there. Look for these techniques whether you are reading fiction or non-fiction – they apply to both.

Have a look at the extract below from 'The Lighthouse' – a short story by the Scottish writer Agnes Owens, in which a sister and brother argue while at the beach.

Bobby stopped to gather shells.

'Throw them away', said Megan. 'You'll get better ones at the lighthouse.'

He emptied his pail then asked if the lighthouse was over there, pointing to the sea wall.

'Don't be stupid. The lighthouse is miles away.'

He said emphatically, 'Then I don't want to go.'

Megan lost her temper. 'If you don't start moving I'll slap your face.'

At that moment, the woman with the dog passed by. 'Is that big girl hitting you?' she asked him.

Before he could speak, Megan had burst out, 'He's my brother and I'll hit him if I want.'

The woman studied them through thoughtful, narrowed eyes. 'Do your parents know you're out here in this lonely place?'

When Megan said they did the woman walked on with the dog, muttering something under her breath which Megan suspected was some kind of threat aimed at her.

She hissed to Bobby, 'See what you've done. For all we know she could be going to report us to the police and you know what that means?'

'What?'

'Mummy and Daddy will be put in jail for neglecting us and I'll have to watch you for ever.'

At that, he let out a howl so loud she was forced to put her hand over his mouth.

'Be quiet, you fool. Do you want that woman back?'

He quietened down when she promised to get him an ice-cream.

'Where's the van?' he asked looking around.

'Over there', she said, pointing in the direction of the lighthouse. At first he believed this, running beside her eagerly, but when they went on for a considerable length without any signs of an ice-cream he began to lag behind...

'If you don't come – ', she began, when he started walking again, and just when she thought he was going to act reasonably for once he stopped in front of a rock.

'Look! There are fish in there,' he said.

Grumbling, she went back to investigate. It was true. There were tiny fish darting about a pool of water within a crevice in the rock.

'Aren't they pretty?' she said, just as he threw a stone into the pool causing them to disappear. She shook him by the shoulders.

'You have to spoil everything, don't you?' she said, letting him go suddenly so that he sat down with a thud. But he was up on his feet quick enough when she said, walking backwards, 'A monster's going to get you one of these days, the way you carry on.'

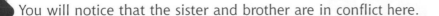

You will notice that the sister and brother are in conflict here.

Pair and Share

Read over the extract and find words or phrases which show how Megan feels about Bobby. Underline them or write them out.

Talk this over with a partner and agree on your decision.

Nearly all the questions on this passage ask about the feelings and attitudes of these two characters (Understanding) and the words the writer uses to describe them (Analysis).

For example, you may be asked to analyse the following words:

don't be stupid

burst out

lost her temper

hissed

you fool

aren't they pretty

grumbling

What do they tell you about Megan? Look also at how Bobby behaves and acts. Again, pick out words to show how he behaves. Would you say he is a typical three year old?

Look more carefully at what each character actually says. How do this brother and sister speak to each other?

The tension in this extract is building up to a tragic outcome – do you think the tension between the two characters (often called **conflict** when we are writing about literature) gets worse as the story progresses? Can you find any evidence for this?

Do not forget about Evaluation questions, though. You may be asked about the **success** of the writing – for example, how successfully the author portrays the sister and brother. Remember that Evaluation questions ask you to give a personal reaction to the writer's work using evidence. Try writing your answer to the question below, using some of the words and phrases from the two-minute task above.

'How successfully does the author portray the sister and brother?'

(Another Evaluation question might be ... **Based on what you have read, what do you think will happen next in the story?** What do you think? A quick clue – the story has a tragic outcome but not the one you would most suspect.)

Target Time

Time to set **your** targets for your Textual Analysis. Refer back to pages 9 and 10 for more information on target setting.

My target is to achieve Grade .... in my Textual Analysis because

....

....

....

To achieve this grade, I am going to work on

....

....

....

Critical Essay

Writing your Critical Essay

This section will help you work towards the Critical Essay you must write in your end of course external exam. And, of course, it will also help you in writing your Personal Study.

The knowledge you now have about Textual Analysis will help you to write this essay. You will have studied parts of a novel or poem or play or mass media text with your teacher. Once you have studied this in enough depth, you will be ready to do a piece of extended writing about it in the exam.

You will have 45 minutes to write your essay.

It is very important that you do not learn an essay off by heart and then copy it out in the exam. If only it was that easy! You must write your essay in response to a question you have not seen before. The good news is that you can be prepared for the essay in other ways by:

- knowing the text really well
- knowing the basic structure to use in your essay (beginning, middle and end)
- having plenty of quotations ready to use.

Worked example: *Of Mice and Men* by John Steinbeck

Your teacher will have discussed with you the texts you can choose from – perhaps you have studied several poems, a play and a novel in class. You will almost certainly have a **favourite** – one you feel most comfortable with. This is the one to choose but only if there is a question that 'fits'!

For now, here is an example – using *Of Mice and Men* by John Steinbeck – that will give you an idea of how to approach your essay.

We are using questions from the prose section of the Intermediate 1 English 2004 external assessment.

> Choose a novel or a short story which has an important turning point that changes things for one of the characters.
>
> Show how the story builds up to the turning point and say why it is important for the character.
>
> In your answer you should refer to such features as: structure, character, or any other appropriate feature.
>
> OR
>
> Choose a novel or a short story or a piece of non-fiction or a group of prose texts which deal with a topic of importance to society.
>
> Say what you learned about the topic from your reading and whether you felt sympathy for the people involved.
>
> In your answer you should refer to such features as: theme, character, or any other appropriate feature.

First things first

Which question would you choose and why?

As soon as you have chosen the question you want to answer, use a highlighter to highlight key words and phrases in the question. For example, in the first question above you might highlight:

- important turning point
- turning point
- structure

- changes things
- important for the character
- character

Try in your essay to concentrate on these key ideas and use them to organise your essay. Plan your writing so that it has a clear structure – in this case, spend some time on explaining how the plot builds up to the turning point, making sure you point out why this is important for the character, and how this changes things for him or her.

Many Intermediate 1 English pupils do not bother with a plan – they start writing without working this out. This may save time but, in the long run, students who plan their writing get better marks because their structure is clearer and more thought out.

Using a mind map is helpful – for this question, put the character's name in the middle of the mind map ('George's turning point') and all your ideas round about it.

Title

You must write a title for your essay that is specific to your text – a good one here would be *An important turning point for George in John Steinbeck's 'Of Mice and Men'*.

Introduction

You should always include an introduction in which you use the key words you have highlighted in the question. Students can be 'stuck' with how to start – simply answer the question as follows ...

In 'Of Mice and Men', George faces a turning point when his friend Lennie is in danger of being killed by a gang of men. After this turning point, George's life changes in every way. The story builds up to this point from the opening pages of the novel when ...

Main body of text

Think of the main body as the filling in a sandwich (the top slice of bread is the introduction and the bottom slice of bread is the conclusion). There is lots more useful advice on writing about literature in the chapter on **'Personal Study: written'**.

You will have to show your knowledge of the text and use quotations in the main body of your essay. Let's practise this.

All the paragraphs in the main body of your writing should contain:

- a point about the text
- evidence from the text (either in your own words or as a quotation)
- a comment about this point.

Use linking words within your paragraph and between paragraphs to make your writing **'flow'**. Here is an example:

> At this point in the novel, Lennie is terrified – although he is still unaware of the crime he has committed. George reassures him – 'gonna get a rabbit', – but the reader knows there can only be one outcome. George must kill Lennie to 'save' him from his own actions.

Conclusion

Finish off with a conclusion which refers back your title and introduction. Here are some key points to include:

- Your conclusion should always mention the key words/ideas again.
- Remind the reader of your intention.
- Summarise the main points of your essay in a general statement at the end.
- Include some 'personal reaction'.
- You can include a quotation – but only if it is relevant and you have not used it earlier!

> The turning point for George in 'Of Mice and Men' is when George realises he will have to 'save' Lennie from his attackers by killing him. The story steadily develops towards this point and my sympathy is with both characters as I have shown. This, for me, was the saddest moment as I realised that both men would never attain the dream of living 'off the fatta the lan' '.

Target Time

To achieve Intermediate 1 English at Grade C in your Critical Essay, you must achieve **all** of the following criteria.

Understanding
Show that you can understand the main ideas in the text by referring to relevant parts of the text.

Analysis
Show that you can analyse in simple terms the structure, style and language of the text.

Evaluation
Show that you have a personal reaction to the text by referring to relevant parts of the text.

Expression
Show that you can express yourself clearly and follow a line of thought. Your spelling, grammar and punctuation must be mainly accurate.

If you want to gain a Grade A, you have to do a little bit more than this.
For Grade A, you must achieve at least three of the following from at least two sections:

Understanding
- Secure understanding of the main points
- Explain important detail

Analysis
- Show some understanding of the writer's literary/linguistic technique (In other words, you must show you understand the writer's style.)

Evaluation
- Show you are being critical about the text (In other words, you must show that you are able to comment on how effective/successful the writer is.)

Expression
- Your expression is consistently clear and establishes a relevant line of thought (In other words, you must show that you are consistently relevant, frequently referring to the key ideas of your essay.)

Your teacher can help explain all this further – and can show you examples of Grade A essays.

Time to set **your** targets for your Critical Essay.
Refer back to pages 9 and 10 for more information on target setting.

My target is to achieve Grade .... in my Critical Essay because

....

....

....

To achieve this grade, I am going to work on

....

....

....

Basic skills
Punctuation

You cannot get good grades in English unless you can punctuate your writing skilfully and correctly.

Why use punctuation?

- When you speak, you punctuate naturally through your pauses and body language.
- However, when you write you have to help your reader understand what you mean through a variety of punctuation marks.
- The more you know about punctuation, the better you will be able to express yourself.
- Pupils who use semi-colons and colons stand out from others, especially if they use these punctuation marks effectively.

Clarify ideas

We need to punctuate our work to help our audience understand us.

Remember that when we let our writing pass into the hands of others, our punctuation marks and the words we use are all that there is to communicate our message. We are no longer in a position to correct any errors, as we would be if we were speaking directly to our audience.

To sum up: **we use punctuation marks to clarify** the points and ideas that we want to communicate to others.

Quick Think

Markers can miss good points and ideas in your writing when their attention is continually drawn to punctuation errors.

Begin all sentences and are used at the beginning of lines of verse.

Are used for **initials of people's names and places**. Remember that 'I' needs a capital letter too.

Are used when you begin **direct speech**; for example: Julia asked, 'Have you begun your revision for English yet?'

Have to be used for adjectives from **proper (specific) nouns**; for example: English, French, Elizabethan and McDonalds.

Capital letters

Need to be used in the **first and main words of titles** of books, newspapers, films, groups and programmes, etc.

Are used when writing letters with 'Dear' and 'Yours . . .'.

Are used for **days of the week, months, holidays** and **special days**.

Are used as **acronyms** for organisations; for example: BBC, NATO and GMTV. Note that you do not need a dot after each letter if it is a well-known organisation.

Quick Think

Get into the habit of proof-reading your work. Target the errors that you usually make.

Two-minute Task

1. Why is punctuation necessary?

2. List four occasions when you would use capital letters.

3. Correct the following sentences:
   a) 'what's the capital of portugal, lauren?'
   b) my favourite song at the moment is 'i knew i loved you' by savage garden.

4. Which words need a capital: hamburger restaurant, monday, summer, the atlantic, westlife, rspca, sea, christmas, louise?

Punctuating sentences

Full stops

A **full stop** is the main punctuation mark that **signals the end of one idea and the beginning of another**.

Sentences help to complete ideas in your writing. You can use full stops to make strong points in your writing, because they slow readers down.

Change your sentences by making some long and some short; **variety** helps to keep your audience interested in what you have to say. Try to be **expressive** through your choice of punctuation.

Read your work aloud and listen to where one idea ends and another begins. Each idea is a sentence. Trust your ears.

Quick Think

Select the punctuation mark that best fits the meaning and purpose. The more expressive you are, the better your writing will be.

Semi-colons

Semi-colons join two or more closely related ideas:

- Steve worked hard for his results; he stuck to his revision plan.
- Spring has come early; the trees have begun to blossom and the grassy banks are full of daffodils.

Semi-colons separate sets of items in a list when there are commas within the sets or lists:

- When you unpack your new computer you will find everything you need: multi-coloured leads; the plugs for your monitor and base unit; the speakers with their leads; a microphone, if this is included, with a stand; manuals for your computer and, if you are lucky, lots of interesting software.

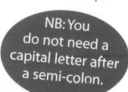

NB: You do not need a capital letter after a semi-colon.

Colons

Colons are two dots, one above the other. They are used to:

- **introduce a list**
  You should bring to your exam: a watch, two pens, a ruler, tissues and hope!

- **introduce quotations**
  Hamlet ponders: 'To be or not to be? That is the question.'

- **expand on the meaning of a previous idea**
  Tracy scored the highest grade in the exam: it was an A.

- **punctuate dialogue in plays**

  Macbeth: If we should fail?
  Lady Macbeth: We fail!
                 But screw your courage to the sticking place, And we'll not fail.

A dash can also do the job of a colon by emphasising the sentence that follows:

- Tom had achieved fantastic results in his exams – he got As in five of them.

Other punctuation

Exclamation marks

Exclamation marks help to express surprise, anger, fear, joy and most other emotions. For example: Louise! It is good to see you!

Question marks

Question marks can be used for **rhetorical questions** where no direct reply is expected, only mental agreement; for example: 'Who could defend a statement like that?'

They can also be used for **requests for information**: 'What time is it?'

You do not need a question mark for an indirect question: 'Siobhan asked me for a pen.'

Quick Think

Look at how professional writers use punctuation as you read their work. Pause over some passages and think about the effectiveness of the punctuation.

Quick Think

To get high grades in Intermediate 1 you will need to vary the length of your sentences and the style of your punctuation. Practise writing sentences of different lengths – longer sentences usually mean more punctuation marks!

Two-minute Task

1. Explain one of the things that semi-colons can do.

2. What does a full stop do?

3. Can a colon introduce a list of items?

4. Can colons be used to introduce a quotation?

5. Give one other purpose for a colon.

Answers 1. They link two closely related phrases or separate sets of items in a list where there are commas within the sets. **2.** It marks the end of a sentence. **3.** Yes. **4.** Yes. **5.** It links another phrase which expands upon the meaning of the first, or punctuates dialogue in plays.

Speech marks and commas

The skilful use of punctuation marks can improve your expression

Commas

Commas separate items in lists:

- I would like three hamburgers, a cheeseburger, a large serving of fries and a coffee.

Commas clarify sentences that could be misleading:

- After a period of calm, students returned after the fire alarm.

> **Quick Think**
>
> Be careful not to use commas instead of full stops in sentences.

Commas need to be used in direct speech:

- Elaine was curious about the previous evening and asked, 'Where did you get to?' 'The shopping centre,' John replied.

Commas can be used to mark off words, phrases and connectives in sentences:

- Billy, who did not like to be made fun of, was angry.
- On the other hand, there was no harm in what Carly said.

Speech marks

There are four main rules for setting out speech:

1. Use **inverted commas** for the words spoken: Catherine said, 'I haven't seen you in ages!'
2. **Direct speech must be separated from the rest of the writing by a punctuation mark**; see the comma in the example above.
3. Remember to **use a capital letter** when you begin the direct speech: Catherine said, 'It's ages since I last saw you.'
4. Each time you introduce a **new speaker**, begin a new line and indent. That is, begin the speech of your new speaker three letter spaces to the right of the margin.

Quotation marks

- Quotation marks are **inverted commas for words or phrases cited from texts**. Use single inverted commas for speech and double inverted commas for speech within speech. For example: *Jane shouted to her husband in the next room, 'Your mother phoned and she said, "When are you going to visit me?"'*

- **Remember to close quotation marks**. It is confusing for readers and markers if you fail to do so! To show that you are ending a quotation, place the final full stop on the outside of the inverted comma; for example: *In My Fair Lady Eliza Doolittle shows her independence from Professor Higgins when she says, 'I can do without you'.*

Eliza Doolittle

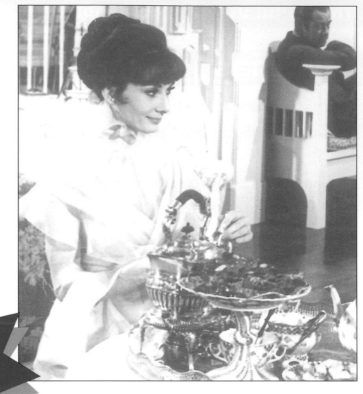

Title marks

- In secondary schools, **inverted commas** are used to signify book titles, stories, newspapers, magazines, television programmes, movies or shows. For example: 'My Fair Lady' is the title of the musical or 1964 film version of the play, 'Pygmalion'.

- In your writing always use inverted commas to show the difference between **characters** and the names of the work in which they appear. For example: Macbeth is a character whereas 'Macbeth' is a play.

Two-minute Task

1. Identify three uses for commas.
2. Make up a sentence in which you use all four rules for setting out speech.
3. What do you need to use when you write out the title of a film, book or story?

Answers 1. They can mark off a list and phrases within a sentence; they are used within direct speech. **2.** Phil said, 'Buy the latest team shirt.' / 'It is too expensive,' said Paul. **3.** Title marks, underlining or italics.

Apostrophes

Apostrophes help to show that something belongs to someone (possession) or to shorten words (contraction).

Key Facts

Its and *it's* can be confusing words.
- If you wrote, 'I emptied a box of its contents', you would not need an apostrophe because *its* in this instance is a possessive pronoun.
- If you say, 'It's going to rain all day', you need an apostrophe because you mean *it is*.

Apostrophes of possession

Possessive pronouns

Pronouns like these do not need apostrophes to show ownership:

- **my**, e.g. The watch is mine.
- **his or hers**, e.g. The computer is hers.
- **yours**, e.g. The bag is yours.
- **its**, e.g. The box was emptied of its contents.
- **ours**, e.g. The car is ours.
- **theirs**, e.g. The house is theirs.

Quick Think

Abbreviated words are only to be used in informal writing. We use them when we speak or write to friends or family. Avoid using shortened words in your assignments and exams unless you are asked to do so.

Apostrophes of ownership for one person or thing

If there is a **single owner, place the apostrophe before the 's'**:

- Tim's video player
- Christine's house

Apostrophes of ownership for more than one owner

If there is **more than one owner**, you need to **put the apostrophe after the 's'** to show that you mean a plural owner:

- The Jacksons' video
- The Smiths' house

If a person's name already ends in 's', you can do one of two things:

- James's haircut or James' haircut

Whichever style you go for, remain consistent.

If a plural noun does not need an 's' to make it plural, you should place your apostrophe before the 's':

- The men's business venture
- The children's playground
- The women's society
- The people's champion

Expression

You can **vary your expression by using an apostrophe**. For example, 'The claws of the cat' becomes 'The cat's claws' with an apostrophe.

If you are unsure of whether to use a possessive apostrophe then write your sentence the long way round. For example, 'Dan's new house' becomes 'The new house of Dan'.

Always ask yourself why you are inserting an apostrophe. Do not put it in just for good measure.

Apostrophes of contraction

Apostrophes are used to show that one or more letters have been missed out.

Contractions combine two words into one with an apostrophe.

- I'm = I am
- They're = They are
- Won't = Will not
- Doesn't = Does not
- Can't = Cannot
- Would've = Would have

Apostrophes when writing the time or dates

- 'I will see Dave at 7 o'clock.' This is the short way of writing 'seven of the clock'.

Missing numbers in dates can be suggested by an apostrophe:

- 21st of September '99
- 3rd of November '01

Apostrophes in plays

Playwrights such as Shakespeare shortened their words to allow their verse to remain in **iambic pentameter**. Shakespeare tried to divide his blank-verse lines into ten syllables, that is, five feet of two syllables each.

Take this example from *Romeo and Juliet*, in which Romeo wants Juliet to exchange vows:

- Romeo: 'Th' exchange of thy love's faithful vow for mine.'

Apostrophes in dialect

Apostrophes are used a great deal by writers when they try to represent local dialect:

- ' 'ow's it goin', me ole mate?'

William Shakespeare

Quick Think

Apostrophes are marks that help readers to understand the intention of the writer. Use them to convey meaning as fully as you can.

Two-minute Task

True or false?

1. Possessive pronouns can take apostrophes.

2. Apostrophes lengthen words.

3. Apostrophes can help to show ownership.

4. If a person's name ends with an 's', you can put the apostrophe after it.

5. I ca'nt is correct.

6. Apostrophes of possession can help to vary your sentences and make them shorter.

Answers 1. False. **2.** False. **3.** True. **4.** True. **5.** False. **6.** True.

Sentences

Sentence types

Sentences can be put into four groups according to what they do. They can be **statements** (which give information), **exclamations** (e.g. My Goodness!), **instructions or commands** (e.g. Insert your card this way up.) or **questions**. Sentences are also grouped into structures: simple, compound, complex and minor.

1. **Simple sentences** must contain:
- **a subject** (what/who does the action)
- **a verb** (the action)

They can have other parts as well, such as:

- **an object** (the person or thing acted upon)
- **a complement** (additional information about the subject)
- **adverbials** (additional information about the verb)

When they form part of other sentences, simple sentences are usually referred to as **clauses**.

2. **Compound sentences join two or more sentences together**. The two parts are joined by **coordinating conjunctions**, such as 'and', 'but' or 'or'. For example: Do you want to catch the bus or will you walk home?

> Look back at page 21 for more information about complex sentences.

3. **Complex sentences** have **two or more clauses joined by subordinating conjunctions**, such as 'although', 'because' or 'if'. The **main clause** makes sense on its own. The **subordinate clause** does not make sense on its own; for example:

> I didn't see you at the party **although** I looked everywhere.

> **If** you read in this light, you'll hurt your eyes.

4. **Minor sentences** usually consist of a single verb or verb phrase. They are often used in instructions or commands, for example: Listen.

Quick Think

Examiners are looking for a variety of sentence styles in your writing. Avoid too many sentences joined by coordinating conjunctions. Remember that short, sharp sentences can be very effective.

The anatomy of a sentence

The **different parts of speech**, such as **noun**, **pronoun**, **adjective**, **verb** and **adverb**, **conjunction** and **preposition**, can be single words or short phrases:

- Old   Alex   walked   slowly.

- Last Wednesday   the   early   train   was derailed   unexpectedly.

It is important to remember that you can only tell what part of speech a word or phrase is when it is in a sentence. For example:

> *London* looks like a noun because it is the name of a place, but in the sentence *I caught the London bus* it is an adjective.

> *Walk* looks like a verb because it is an action, but in the sentence *They went for a walk* it is a noun.

Variety within sentences

As well as using all the different sentence types, you will impress examiners if you **vary the internal structure of your sentences**. Two ways of doing this involve:

- placing the most important information at the beginning of the sentence
- withholding important information until the end to create suspense.

For example: *Passing my driving test was probably one of the proudest moments of my life* places emphasis on the passing of the test; whereas *One of the proudest moments of my life was probably passing my driving test* uses exactly the same words but places the emphasis on how the speaker felt.

Two-minute Task

True or false?

1. Independent clauses can make sense on their own.
2. 'When you look into them' is a sentence.
3. The sentence, 'Write your name in block capitals' is a statement.
4. Varying your sentences can improve your expression.

Answers 1. True. **2.** True. **3.** False: it is a command or an instruction. **4.** True.

Spellings

Methods of learning tricky spellings

1. Look up words in **dictionaries** and check their spellings. Dictionaries work on the alphabet principle for each word and finding words becomes easier with practice. Carry a small dictionary with you. Relying on teachers and others to spell words for you means that you will never really learn them. Aim to be an independent learner.

2. The **Look–Say–Cover–Write–Check** method is successful as long as you have spelled the word correctly in the first place. Learning words by repeating this process does work.

3. Try writing a crazy but **memorable sentence** using each letter of the word (a **mnemonic**). For example, a mnemonic for the word believe could be: *Big Elephants Look Inside Elephantine Vases Everywhere*. However, only use this method for the few words that are the biggest problems for you, otherwise you will have too many strange phrases to remember.

4. Use the **sound of words** to help you spell them. Work your way through each syllable as you aim to spell the word. This works for many words and is always worth trying before using other methods.

5. For **tricky plural endings**:
   - If a noun ends with a 'y' and it has a letter such as 't', 'r' or 'n' before the 'y', you need to add 'ies' to the plural. For example: **diary – diaries**; **curry – curries**; **company – companies**; **city – cities**.
   - If the last letter before the 'y' is a vowel (a, e, i, o, u) you have to add an 's' to make the plural. For example: **boy – boys**; **journey – journeys**; **key – keys**; **guy – guys**; **monkey – monkeys**.
   - Words which end in 'fe', such as *knife*, take 'ves' in plurals; similarly, words ending in 'f', like *shelf* or *half*, change to *shelves* and *halves* in plurals.

6. Use **'i' before 'e' except after 'c'**; for example; *thief* and *sieve*, but *receive*.

7. **Proof-read** your work for words that you are likely to spell incorrectly. Make a list of these words from a number of subjects and focus on learning them.

Structures

Connective words link phrases, sentences and paragraphs together.

Ordering your ideas

Words that help to put your ideas in order
- *firstly, then, so far, secondly, in the end, next, eventually, subsequently, at last, at length, afterwards*

Words for exceptions
- *only, if, unless, except (for), save for*

Quick Think
The skilful use of **connectives** can help you to vary your sentence structure and improve your style.

Making points and giving examples

Words used to argue and make points
- *consequently, thus, so, as a result, because, as, hence, therefore, since, until, whenever, accordingly, as long as*

Words to help you give examples
- *for example, for instance, such as, take the case of, thus, as (evidence), to show that, as revealed by*

Words for extra points or ideas
- *and, too, what is more, also, furthermore, and then, again, moreover, as well as, in addition*

Words to emphasise points
- *above all, in particular, notably, specifically, indeed, more important, especially, significant(ly), in fact*

in addition
take the case of
as a result
above all
therefore

Paragraphing

Paragraphs are necessary to break the text flow and help the reader to follow the writer's meaning.

- Paragraphs are **groups of sentences connected by the same topic**. Each paragraph carries a main idea.
- The main sentence of a paragraph is often found at the beginning and it is called a **topic sentence**. For example: *Successful students plan their revision in each subject. They plan how much time they have available and then try to cover a number of areas in each subject.*
- Any paragraphs following the first paragraph will need to **begin on a new line, indented 2 cm from the page margin**.
- You can link your paragraphs together skilfully by using the **connecting words** found in the boxes on these pages.

Being persuasive and analytical

Words to persuade

- *of course, naturally, obviously, clearly, certainly, surely, evidently*

Words to help you show an opinion or analyse

- *it would seem, to suggest, one might conclude/propose/deduce/infer/imply/ say/consider*

Comparing and contrasting

Words to make a contrast or show what is different

- *but, nevertheless, alternatively, despite this, on the contrary, however, yet, the opposite, instead, whereas, to turn to, although, still, on the other hand*

Words to compare things in your writing or show what is similar

- *equally, in the same way, as with, likewise, similarly, compared with, an equivalent*

Essay endings

Words to sum up or end with

- *in brief, in summary, throughout, in all, on the whole, to sum up, overall, finally, to conclude, to recap, in the end*

in summary
on the whole
to conclude

Quick Think

Use appropriate and varied connective words in your essays to signpost your arguments.

Two-minute Task

1. Why use paragraphs?

2. Identify two words that can help you to compare pieces of writing.

3. What is the difference between *comparing* and *contrasting*?

4. Give two words that help to emphasise points in writing.

5. What do the words *furthermore* and *moreover* help you to do?

Answers 1. Paragraphs help readers to follow your ideas. They also break up the text according to topics. **2.** Any of the following: *in the same way, similarly, equally, as with, likewise, compared with, an equivalent.* **3.** To compare is to look for similarities and to contrast is to look for differences. **4.** Any of the following: *indeed, in particular, above all, notably, specifically, more importantly, especially, significantly, in fact.* **5.** They help you to make extra points or ideas.

Improve your style

Control

Teachers and examiners are looking for control in your writing. This means an awareness of the effect that **different writing techniques** can have and **deliberate use of them**.

Vocabulary and choice of words

The words you choose need to be **appropriate** for the task and as **accurate** as possible. For example, does your character get into a car, a battered old Ford, a people carrier or an oversized all-terrain vehicle? Do characters 'say' things all the time or do they 'mutter', 'mumble' or 'shout'?

Varying sentences and paragraphs

You already know about using different types of sentences, but you should also think about the **rhythm of your writing**. Large stretches of **long sentences can create a sense of continuity and flow**, but they can also become monotonous. **Try short sentences for emphasis**. Even more emphatic than the short sentence is the short paragraph.

A single sentence paragraph really stands out.

You can build up tension by using short, snappy sentences that make the reader pause over each detail:

'I ran. Ran for all I was worth! Sometimes I stumbled over tree roots. Branches slashed my face. Something was rapidly hunting me down. Twigs and branches snapped in the desperate rushing behind me. A savage, wolf-like howl tore the air. Something clasped my leg! "God help me!" I screamed, as I gasped for breath.'

Descriptive writing

The power of descriptive writing comes in the **accurate choice of nouns and verbs**. Adjectives and adverbs can help to pin down what you say even more accurately. Always make sure that your adjectives or adverbs are doing some work. For example, *he walked slowly* could be conveyed with the single verb *he strolled*; *a gnarled oak* will create a much clearer picture in your readers' minds than *a big twisted tree*. Finally, remember to **appeal to all five senses in descriptive writing**.

Some pitfalls to avoid

- Do not confuse big words with a sophisticated style. Remember that you want to give your readers as clear a picture as possible.
- Do not overdo any one effect. If all your sentences have an unusual structure, people will find it distracting.
- Use figurative language sparingly. One well-chosen simile or metaphor will stand out like a rose in a desert.

Varying sentence structures

The first part of a sentence tends to contain the subject. In the middle of the sentence there is often known information – the new information comes at the end. From time to time you can vary this order. Compare the impact of: *As I put the car into gear the engine went 'thunk'* with *'Thunk' went the engine as I put the car into gear.*

You also have a great deal of choice when it comes to the placing of **adverbial phrases**. These tell you about things like time, mood and manner. For example:

- *With deliberate slowness,* Dr Shrike marked out the area he was going to cut.
- Dr Shrike, *with deliberate slowness,* marked out the area he was going to cut.
- Dr Shrike marked out the area he was going to cut *with deliberate slowness.*

Quick Think

A clear, fluent, written style is something that you are going to have to work at. Examine the style of the writers you are studying and think about phrases, words and punctuation that could work for you.

How to improve your expression

Clarity and brevity

- Keep what you write **brief**, **simple** and **clear**.
- **Avoid long-winded, pompous sentences**; for example: *I remained in my abode and passed the time watching uninteresting programmes while looking at the little box in the corner.* This is tedious; try this instead: *I stayed at home watching boring programmes on TV.*

Clichés

Clichés are **tired expressions and imagery** that have **lost impact because of overuse**. Avoid the following:

like the plague   *like two ships that pass in the night*
food for thought   *leaves much to be desired*

> ### Quick Think
> Try to improve your expression as you develop the habit of proof-reading your work. The Russian writer Chekhov said, 'Rewrite everything five times!'

Writing effective sentences

In a stylish, effective sentence:

- the beginning is the second-most important part;
- the middle is the least important part;
- the end is the most important part.

Take, for example, this line from Shakespeare's *Twelfth Night*:
'Some are born great, some achieve greatness and some have greatness thrust upon 'em.'

Avoid overworked words because they can be boring and repetitive, e.g. got, get, nice, good, totally, a lot of, kind of.

Avoid using tautologies – that is, repeating yourself unnecessarily, e.g. final end, sad misfortune, puzzling mystery.

Also try to **avoid reinforcing words** with words that would be better left out; your writing will have more impact without them. Word-reinforcement to avoid includes: totally wrong, absolutely fantastic, seriously consider.

Circumlocutions

Circumlocutions are **roundabout ways of saying things**. Again, stick to simple words or expressions, as these are usually more effective:

- in a majority of cases = usually
- in the event that = if
- owing to the fact that = because
- in less than no time = quickly
- on the grounds that = because
- with the exception of = except.

Two-minute Task

1. Reduce these phrases to one word:
   a) due to the fact that
   b) pink in colour
   c) in this day and age.

2. What is the danger of overdoing description?

3. Identify a cliché and explain why you should try to avoid clichés in your writing.

Answers 1. a) because; **b)** pink; **c)** now. **2.** The readers could lose sight of your meaning. **3.** There are numerous examples of clichés; for example, 'Shot in the foot'. The image has no impact and will simply pass readers by, or worse, bore them.

Start writing!

Learning Outcome 2 of the Language Study is usually the part of Intermediate 1 English that students enjoy most – in this unit, you are allowed to write in any way you like on any topic you like! Try each of the three main types of writing (**expressive**, **personal**, **functional**), then talk to your teacher about which one is for you.

Unless you write a poem, you must write a minimum of 300 words. You must achieve all the performance criteria listed in the **'Target Time'** section within the one piece of writing to gain your Intermediate 1.

The writing process

You will write your piece in school/college but a lot of the work on this will be done independently. You can 'check in' with your teacher when necessary. Your teacher will tell you about the stages and deadlines involved, but here is a basic summary of the writing process.

Draft title    First, you must submit a draft title to your teacher.

Proposal    You have to make clear what your intention (sometimes called a **proposal**) is at the start. Your intention might be to explain an event that changed your life or to argue against animal testing or to create a terrifying horror story or to write a set of love poems – it is up to you!

Rough plan    An outline of the **'shape'** of your writing, usually a paragraph plan.

Rough draft    A rough version of your writing to be discussed with your teacher.

Final version    The final writing, written in school/college on a specified date.

Do not throw out any of your rough work – keep all your plans and rough work as evidence – although only the final piece of writing is assessed.

Genres

There are hundreds of different genres or types of writing in English – look at the list below. Beside each one are the 'conventions' of the genre. 'Conventions' are the language and layout 'clues' that tell you what type of text you are reading.

Two-minute Task

Think about each of the genres and their 'conventions' or clues listed below. Can you add in any of the 'conventions' for the genre that is left blank?

Genre	Convention
love story	'romantic' language, theme of love
recipe	list of ingredients, instructions, specialist vocabulary such as tbsp.
spy story	'adventure' theme, quick action, technical vocabulary
newspaper article	

You can choose to do any type of writing from the following genres:

- **Expressive**
- **Creative**
- **Report.**

You must write a **minimum of 300 words** unless you write a poem (which can be of any length as long as the length suits your purpose).

Discuss with your teacher which of these types of writing is the best one for you. That way, you can concentrate on improving your skills in that specific genre.

Expressive writing

The **expressive** genre includes the following three types of writing and you can choose from any one of them:

- a **personal reflective** essay
- a **persuasive** essay
- an **argumentative** essay.

The sections that follow explain each of these in more detail.

Your main purpose in this genre is to **entertain.** (There is more on **purpose** in the **'Reading'** chapter of the book.) Make your writing funny, interesting, heart-breaking, angry – go for it! Just don't make it boring!

Personal reflective writing

Personal reflective writing means **writing about your reaction to something that has happened to you**. It is usually about one single idea or experience and will always include reflection on what has happened and your feelings about it.

This reflection is what makes the writing interesting – otherwise, your essay will become just another account of someone breaking a leg or entering a cheer-leading competition. It is your thoughts and feelings about the experience that will make your writing original and fresh.

Two-minute Task

Study the two passages below, then decide which one is more effective, and why. Note down the phrases in both passages that show how the writer has reflected on his experience.

I woke up in hospital with my leg all in plaster. It was really sore and it was itchy too. My mum and dad came to fetch me after about a day, and I went back to school the next week ...

I woke up – to my surprise – in hospital! What a shock to see my leg all covered in plaster. It was really sore, and I tried not to cry all day. I remember when I think back that it was the itching that really got to me – not the pain. I was so glad to see my mum and dad when they came to fetch me the next day. It was difficult going back to school with everyone staring at me and not being able to move easily because of the crutches ...

The other thing to remember when writing about personal experience is that you must describe the incident or experience in an **interesting** way – use describing words and phrases. Again, this is what will make your writing stand out. You will probably write your essay in chronological order – this means in the order that things happened to you. This can sometimes lead to very dull writing – 'Then I did this, then I did that. Then he said, then she said ...' and so on.

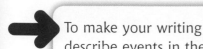

To make your writing more interesting, you could use **flashbacks** or perhaps describe events in the **past tense** and add a section at the end describing your thoughts as you reflect back on events now.

Another way to improve this is to use interesting words and phrases.

Pair and Share

Look at the following phrases. Discuss with your partner how to rewrite them and make them more interesting – the first one is done for you.

I fell on the floor and hurt my ankle.

I tumbled towards the floor, crashing down onto my ankle with

a snap and a shocking pain up my leg.

My teacher was smiling.

....

....

I won the contest.

....

....

I could not sleep.

....

....

My gran held my hand.

....

....

Remember to plan your writing as usual. Think of an effective title. Which is better: *My First Holiday Abroad* or *Florida – my 'highs and lows'*?

Don't forget this is **personal** writing – you will have succeeded if the reader feels involved in your story and has a good idea of the type of person you are after reading the essay! To put this across, explain clearly how you were affected by the experience and how you felt about it afterwards – the **'reflective'** part of the writing. Go into detail about what you learned, perhaps saying how you would do things differently now you are older.

Lastly, **never** make up a personal experience. If you have not genuinely had the experience, reacted to it and reflected on it, this will be very clear to the reader and will result in dull writing that does not 'ring true'. Your emotions must be genuine.

Persuasive writing

What is persuasive writing? In persuasive writing, you must:

- explain your point of view
- try to persuade the reader about your point of view.

Your **purpose** in this type of writing is to **influence** your reader's **opinion.** Spend some time researching your topic so that you are armed with facts, statistics and examples to use in your final writing.

Persuasive writing usually begins with a clear statement of your point of view, for example, 'Fox hunting is a cruel and outdated way of keeping fox numbers down'.

- You must write in a logical order.
- Each point you make must have evidence to back it up.
- You must write formally.

Persuasive writing usually ends with a clear summary of your point of view.

Your writing must show a clear belief or conviction about your topic. If you do not feel genuinely strongly about a topic, there is little point in writing about it. You will not sound convincing and your writing will quickly become boring to read. Remember that you can present your work in any suitable way – you could design a leaflet or newsletter for a campaign against fox hunting, for example, rather than a straightforward essay. Always discuss your ideas with your teacher first.

Another type of persuasive writing is writing to persuade the reader to **buy** something – that is, an **advertisement**.

For all types of persuasive writing, you must use at least some of the **techniques** below.

Rhetorical questions

These are questions which make the reader think. Because there is no answer provided, the reader must provide his or her own answer. This is a technique which is frequently used in advertisements.

'Need a holiday?'

'Ever thought of changing your car?'

Formal/informal language

Many advertisements use informal language so that they appeal to as wide a range of potential customers as possible. In persuasive essays, however, you should write as formally as you can – although you can use informal words for effect (refer to the **'Close Reading'** section for more information on formal and informal words).

'Gotcha!'

'This all-weather jacket is the bee's knees.'

'Emotive' language

'Emotive' simply means causing emotion – that is to say, using strong words which will cause a certain emotion in the reader. Remember this example from the **'Reading'** chapter? The writer uses emotive, strong language to make the reader disgusted and horrified at the idea of fox hunting.

Two-minute Task

It makes my blood boil! Terrified foxes, running in terror from those bloodthirsty hounds! I am aware that foxes have to be culled, but hunting turns fox killing into a game and that is surely not right!

Can you pick out the emotive words and phrases?

In an advertisement, use emotive words to create a mood or an image for a product. For example, words such as 'special', 'exotic' and 'magical' create the idea of luxury in the reader's mind.

Two-minute Task

If you want to write persuasively, which type would you prefer to write and why – an advertisement or a piece of writing persuading your reader about a topic?

Argumentative writing

In an **argumentative essay**, you present an argument on a topic or issue.

You must state your point of view clearly at the beginning and at the end so that the reader is in no doubt about your chosen point of view. You should mention arguments for the other 'side' but when you do this, you must argue **against** them as strongly as you have argued **for** your own 'side'.

You will:

- research your topic to find facts, statistics and examples
- organise your writing well
- write in a reasonable way with conviction but without exaggerating
- develop your essay by giving examples and evidence and working towards a clear conclusion
- compare and contrast ideas for the two 'sides' of your topic
- come to a clear conclusion at the end.

Fast food is bad for you!

Fast food is responsible for … Secondly … Furthermore … for example … on the other hand … however … even though … but … despite … finally

Quick Think

Have you read any magazine articles or editorials in newspapers recently that you have strongly agreed or disagreed with? Think about how they managed to achieve this.

Examples/evidence

Your evidence must be correct – do thorough research on the internet, in newspapers and in encyclopaedias – so that your facts and figures are accurate and up-to-date. There is advice on researching in the **'Reading'** chapter under 'Basic skills')

Planning

Plan your writing – this is **crucial** if you are writing an argumentative essay. Your writing must be well structured. Look at the plan below:

Introduction	State your intention and your attitude clearly.
Section 1	Make your first point with evidence.
Section 2	Make your second point with evidence.
Section 3	Make your third point with evidence.
Section 4	Give an opposing view and argue against it.
Section 5	Give another opposing view and argue against it.
Conclusion	State your point of view clearly and summarise the main reasons for this.

In **persuasive writing**, it is important that you feel very strongly about the topic, so choose a topic you feel strongly about, whether it be the use of drugs in sport, the Royal family, vegetarianism, private schools or whatever. In **argumentative writing**, however, you do not have to feel strongly about the topic – you are simply looking carefully at both sides of an argument, without strong personal feelings.

Pair and Share

If you choose the Expressive Writing genre, would you choose to write:

- a personal reflective essay
- a persuasive essay
- an argumentative essay?

Talk this over with a partner and agree on your decision.

Creative writing

The **creative genre** includes the following three types of writing and you can choose from any one of these:

- a piece of prose fiction
- a drama script
- a poem or poems (linked by theme)

The sections that follow explain each of these in more detail. Your main purpose in this genre is to **entertain.** (There is more on **purpose** in the 'Reading' chapter of the book.)

Prose fiction

The most popular form of writing is **prose fiction** – for example, a chapter from a novel or a short story. Stories can take thousands of different forms. Choose a genre; then begin to plan. Do you want to write a comedy or a horror story? A mystery or a romance? A story based in the future, or on another planet?

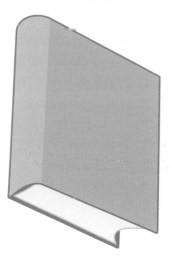

Use this checklist as you plan your writing.

Setting	Is your story in the past or present or future? Where and when does it take place? Is it based on a real life event or is it pure fantasy?
Character	Who are the main and minor characters? How will you establish them at the beginning of the story? Build up a profile for each character – name (choose carefully!), age, appearance, personality, background and so on.
Narrator	Who will 'tell the story'? Will you write in the first or third person?
Plot	What will happen? How will the characters and events develop? What will be the 'high point'?

Opening	What will the opening be? A description? One word? A piece of dialogue? Might your story begin in the middle of an event or crisis?
Theme	What will your story be about? Conflict? Love? The future? Childhood? Prejudice? Memory?
Dialogue	Will you include dialogue? How will the characters speak?
Description	How will you describe the characters, places, situations? Through the five senses – touch, taste, sight, smell, sound?
Tone	Will your story be funny, sad, serious, thought-provoking?

Now plan your writing as usual – a mind map might be useful here. Put the title of your story in the middle of the page and write all your ideas round about it. Let your imagination run away with you … and enjoy writing.

Pair and Share

Look at the openings below – which would you choose and why?

Talk this over with a partner and agree on your decision.

Imagine. Imagine the sound of the train on the tracks. Imagine the smell of the damp carriage. Imagine the frayed velvet seats, springs all broken. Imagine. The conductor wheezes along and …

Lord Lockyer jumped to his feet and clutched at the railing with white knuckles. 'This is a travesty of justice!' he shouted at the jury. 'I must protest my innocence!' …

Aneesh walked through the turnstile, pushing quickly as she always did, not liking the feeling of being imprisoned in some sort of cage. She could smell the chlorine from the pool before she saw the glassy blue water. Would he be here so early? The air was still as silence as she entered the baths …

Why not try writing a story using one of these openings? Remember to plan a shape for your story and check this out with the teacher as you go along. All the usual rules apply, of course. Punctuate and spell correctly and make sure your story has a clear structure. Why not try an unusual structure – like telling the reader at the beginning of a murder mystery 'whodunnit'. Or you might want to spring a surprising ending on the reader!

One thing to remember in writing both prose fiction and drama (in the next section) is that almost all fiction and drama writing deals with **conflict**. This does not mean your characters have to fight each other or have battles – it simply means that characters can disagree with each other. Or perhaps there is a conflict because two characters are not in love with each other. In thrillers or murder mysteries, the conflict is obvious – someone has been murdered!

'Internal conflict' is very important – characters may have a dilemma or issue within themselves that they have to overcome.

You may find it helpful to think about conflict as 'tension' – an idea or issue or problem that will be resolved at the end of the story or drama. Remember the conflict between Bobby and Megan in 'The Lighthouse' story on page 34?

Drama

If you choose **drama** writing for your assessment you may only have time to write a **short scene** or **monologue** (one character 'telling the story'). Perhaps you could make clear that you are writing the opening scene or the closing monologue of a longer play?

To show it is an opening scene, include the title of the play. Perhaps you could use the phrase Act One, Scene One and/or write a description of what the stage set looks like as this is normally done at the very beginning of a play. To make it look really professional, add a list of all the characters (called 'Dramatis Personae') although not all of these characters might appear in the first scene.

If you are writing the closing scene of a play, it is important to let the reader/examiner know what has happened earlier on in the play. Add this at the beginning of your writing before you launch in!

Look in the box below for important things to remember when creating dramatic characters.

Set out your script correctly – the introduction should be followed by characters' names on the left hand side. Insert a new line each time a new character speaks and remember that there is no need for inverted commas
Create believable characters who are interesting and with whom the reader can sympathise or get angry or become impatient – the reader **must** care about the characters in some way.
The dialogue (or 'speech') that the characters say is crucial in that it helps the reader to understand the characters. Build up a profile for each character before you start: name (choose carefully!), age, appearance, personality, background, speech and so on. Think about the first time they will appear in the drama – how will you establish what they are like?

Two-minute Task

Think about the following characters – in some cases you have the name only and in some a character description. Can you complete the table with appropriate names, ages and descriptions?

Name	Description	Age
Lord Rupert Tempest		
	A young, dark skinned girl, possibly a gypsy, very unkempt and uncared for …	
Kim Kitchener		

Don't forget the following!

- Include stage directions (written in brackets between pieces of dialogue) about how the character should move, gesture, talk and so on. Note any lighting, special effects, etc.
- Create an atmosphere – what mood do you want? Develop characters, plot, theme, setting to convey this mood.

Watch as many plays as you can to learn about how dramatists create dramas – all of them will give you insights and ideas.

Poem or a set of linked poems

You can write one poem or a set of poems that have the same theme, or are linked. There is no set length for a poem – the length should be 'appropriate to the purpose'. This means that if your poem is a brief 'snapshot' of a moment, it might not necessarily be very long. However, if you want to write a narrative poem about an event or set of events, this might be longer.

The great thing about poetry is that there are very few 'rules'. The famous American poet e e cummings, for example, never used punctuation! You can miss out any punctuation, place words anywhere on the page, create strange and unusual words or word order. If you are very imaginative, this is the writing for you!

You do need to make some decisions though: poetry is not just a random collection of words. Poets make very careful deliberate choices about which words to use and where to place them. Here are some things that poets can do:

- choose words
- choose patterns of words and images
- arrange words carefully
- choose length and pattern of lines
- choose length and pattern of verses
- make surprising connections between words
- use 'strong' words full of associations
- use imagery
- use sounds for effect
- choose a rhythm
- choose whether to use rhyme
- use unusual grammar or punctuation.

A poem should always be original – it should present the reader with a new way of looking at something or present a new idea in a striking way. A poem should also have a clear theme. If you are writing a set of poems on the same theme, make sure your theme is crystal clear – perhaps each of the poems could deal with a different aspect of the theme? Could the poems have linked titles or start or end in the same way? Could they all have the same format or could they look at the same theme through different 'eyes'?

Two-minute Task

The Japanese form of poetry writing – haiku – is very good practice for choosing exactly the right word and placing it in exactly the right place. Haiku usually have five syllables in the first line, seven in the middle line and five in the last line. Do all the haiku here by Alan Spence follow this rule?

the puppy ferociously challenging a daffodil	cold rain at the window the only child scolds her doll
using a peach for a paperweight – summer breeze	I know I will die but still ... the full round moon

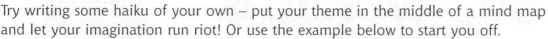

Try writing some haiku of your own – put your theme in the middle of a mind map and let your imagination run riot! Or use the example below to start you off.

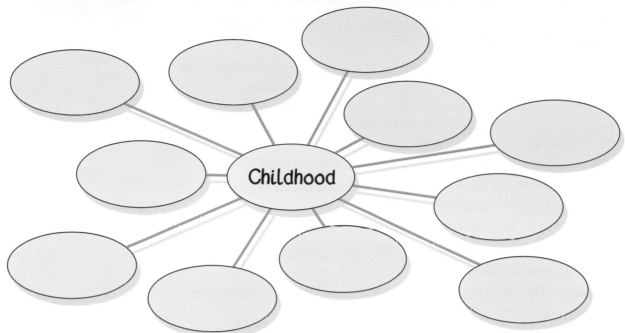

Haikus are very simple poems – they are very short and quite straightforward to write! What about attempting something different? You could write a sonnet (sonnets have 14 lines, usually divided into two verses of 8 lines then 6 lines) or a ballad (a poem which can be spoken or sung) or an epic poem or an ode …

Ask your teacher for help in finding out about all these different types – they will give you inspiration and ideas.

Have a look at the cover of this book – this famous poem was the inspiration for it! The poem, by Robert Burns, is in a very traditional form – four verses with four lines in each with lines 2 and 4 rhyming. It also uses Scottish vocabulary – words and phrases like 'bonnie lass' and 'seas gang dry'. Do you want to write a Scottish poem, perhaps including words used in your area of Scotland?

You could write a descriptive poem about a place only you know well, using words you know well. That would be truly original poetry!

Oh my luve is like a red, red rose
That's newly sprung in June:
Oh my luve is like a melodie,
That's sweetly play'd in tune.

As fair art thou, my bonnie lass,
So deep in luve am I;
And I will luve thee still, my dear,
Till a' the seas gang dry.

Till a' the seas gang dry, my dear,
And the rocks melt wi' the sun:
And I will luve thee still, my dear,
While the sands o' life shall run.

And fare thee weel, my only luve!
And fare thee weel a while!
And I will come again, my luve,
Tho it were ten thousand mile!

As before, the more poetry you read, the better. Try reading poetry from other centuries and countries to get an idea of the huge variety of forms you can choose from. Poetry is the type of writing to go for if you love words and 'playing' with words. The best poetry is made up of original ideas – and phrases that no-one has ever thought of putting together before!

Report writing

Finally, you can choose a completely different type of writing if you wish. This is **report writing.**

First, choose the topic for your report – this might be homelessness or single sex schools or football hooliganism or a topic which you might be studying elsewhere in school/college. You must read at least **three** sources of information about this topic. You will probably find you have a large collection of information such as leaflets, articles, diagrams/graphs and programmes to choose from.

Once you have chosen your topic, your teacher will advise you about where to find information. It may be that you can use material from another subject which you have already researched.

Your task is to read through all the information, take notes and then write up the information in your own words.

In discussion with your teacher, think how to present this information. Your report must:

- have a purpose – for example, to convey information on a topic. You should state this somewhere in your writing, for example,
  This information leaflet will summarise the options for those who choose to leave school at aged 16.
- be well organised with a clear structure
- use headings, charts, etc. if appropriate
- use bullet points, numbering, lists if appropriate
- use appropriate language and tone – reports are usually impersonal and formal and **never** include the personal opinions of the writer.

Your teacher will give you practice in writing reports. Reading textbooks and non-fiction information books and texts will help you. An example task is given below.

Pair and Share

Your task is to read through the sources given, take notes about the ideas in them, then write up a report in your own words on **Vegetarianism for Children**. There are three sources here although you would normally have much more information than this.

Remember – try not to use the writers' words. Change the information into your own words.

Talk this over with your partner and agree on your decisions.

Source one

Eating Green

I crunch into a carrot
Taste the earth and sweet juice
I want to soothe animals, not
kill them.
Care for living creatures, do not torture them.
I do not hurt the tomato as I pick it from its branch and smell its fragrance.
As I admire its ruby orange shine.
I bite into an apple
Taste the flesh and pips.
A taste of health.

Source two

> **Food and Drink Federation** *April 2003*
> A poll of 1003 adults.
> 7% of those polled claimed to be vegetarian.
> Two thirds had eaten a meatless meal in 2003

Source three

Kids, food and health

Adapted from *Veggie Life*, May 1994

If you're wondering whether a vegetarian diet is the healthiest choice for your growing child—rest assured. A variety of studies have shown that the standard American meat-and-dairy-centered diet is laden with saturated fats, and is low in fibre and excessively high in protein. This diet begins to clog the arteries in childhood, and puts our children on the road to heart attacks, strokes, cancer and obesity.

A study published in the May 1987 issue of the *American Journal of Diseases of Children* reported that obesity in children is rising at an alarming rate: 54 percent increase in 6- to 11-year-olds and 39 percent increase in 12- to 17-year-olds since 1960.

Breakfast is often a cereal whose first few ingredients are some form of sugar. The average school lunch derives 39 percent of its calories from fat. Dinner, prepared quickly by work-weary parents, is all too often hamburgers, pizza or defrosted fried chicken accompanied by refined white bread.

Not surprisingly, surveys have shown that the typical American diet results not only in over consumption of calories, fat, cholesterol and sodium, but in inadequate intake of essential nutrients as well. More than 50 percent of 2- to 10-year-olds are currently thought to have inadequate intakes of iron, calcium, B6, zinc and magnesium.

A low fat, whole food vegetarian diet can easily provide your child adequate protein and a healthy supply of fibre, vitamins and minerals, including those (such as iron, calcium, zinc, magnesium and B6) that are often found lacking in the diets of so many children.

By Lara Pizzorno, M.A., L.M.P. and Joe Pizzorno, N.D

Pair and Share

Finally, think about all the types of writing you have read about in this chapter:

- Expressive
- Creative
- Report

Which would you choose? Talk this over with a partner and agree on your decision.

Target Time

Whatever type of writing you choose, you must achieve all of the following criteria in your final assessment. It is important to realise that you have to achieve **all** of these criteria – in other words, you will not pass if you do well in the first three but use very poor spelling, grammar and punctuation!

content
Content is mainly relevant and appropriate.
There is an attempt to develop a number of ideas.

structure
The writing is organised in a straightforward and appropriate structure.

expression
There is use of basic techniques such as accurate word choice and variety in sentence structure and an appropriate tone.

technical accuracy
Spelling, grammar and punctuation are mainly accurate.

Time to set **your** targets for writing. Refer back to pages 9 and 10 for more information on target setting.

My target is to achieve Grade .... in my Writing because

....

....

....

To achieve this grade, I am going to work on

....

....

....

What's it all about?

This unit is all about your **written Personal Study** and how to tackle it. There is an option to do a **spoken** presentation for your Personal Study and there is further advice on this in the **'Personal Study: spoken'** chapter. But even if you are going to do a spoken presentation for your Personal Study, you should read this section first! This section gives you advice on:

- choosing a text or topic
- writing a title
- writing your intention or proposal
- organising your writing
- how to write about a text
- how to write about a topic
- conclusion

The Personal Study is a piece of writing on an aspect (or aspects) of a **text** (or **texts**) or of a **topic** (or **topics**). You should study this text or topic on your own, although your teacher will advise you on your choice. Your teacher must approve of your choice before you even start!

The essay must be **your** independent work and not on a text(s) or topic(s) you have studied in class. Again, check this out with your teacher if you are not sure.

Your independent work will be supervised by your teacher but it will not be taught by your teacher in the same way as, for example, how to punctuate sentences or how to answer questions on a Close Reading passage. Your teacher is not allowed to give you notes or teach the class or tell you what text to choose or what to write! The Personal Study is all about you working on your own – your teacher is there to help and guide you but researching, planning and writing the essay are all up to you.

Whether you are doing a written or spoken Personal Study, there will be plenty of opportunities in class for group discussion and to make presentations to each other. This really is a great way to learn and will equip you with invaluable skills for life!

You will discuss what you want to do with your teacher and then submit the stages below as and when appropriate. Your teacher will tell you the deadline dates for each of these stages:

- a title for your writing
- a proposal for your writing
- a plan of your writing
- a first draft of your writing
- a final draft of your writing.

Your review will be a **minimum of 500** words.

The final draft of your writing will be done in class in **one** hour. You can take in your text, your outline and any of your own notes (but not more than two pages).

Choosing your text or topic

You can choose any text or topic that you like, although your teacher will help you to choose something appropriate. Most pupils choose to write about a text – a novel, play, poem or non-fiction writing such as autobiography or journalism. You can write about a film or other media text. You may prefer to compare two texts instead of writing about just one. If you want to do a comparison, your teacher will help you with the structure of your writing.

You might want to choose a language topic – for example, the language of advertising or the language used in sport. You could analyse how writers write about a particular topic which you have researched in depth, e.g. travel or homelessness.

You choose!

Quick Think

Would you prefer to write about a text or a topic for your Personal Study?

If a text, do you have one in mind?

If a topic, do you have one in mind?

If your brain hurts and you can't think of anything, talk to your teacher. Start reading anything and everything – newspapers, adverts, books, etc. Start watching and listening critically to films or TV programmes. Get down to your local library or school/college library for inspiration!

Here are some ideas for modern fiction texts that you might like to consider. Most will be in your school/college or local library.

Billy Elliot	Melvin Burgess
Junk	Melvin Burgess
Heroes	Robert Cormier
I am the Cheese	Robert Cormier
The Outsiders	S E Hinton
Horowitz Horror	Anthony Horowitz
Carrie	Stephen King
Chinese Cinderella	Adeline Mah
A Child Called It	Dave Peltzer
Holes	Louis Sachar
Cirque du Freak	Darren Shan
Stone Cold	Robert Swindells
Secret Diary of Adrian Mole	Sue Townsend
Refugee Boy	Benjamin Zephaniah

Title

You have chosen your text or topic and you have read and researched and found information and taken notes. (Look back at Basic Skills in the 'Reading' chapter for advice. Also, later in this section there is more help on **Taking Notes.**) So far, so good. You now have to submit a draft title to your teacher. Your title is much more important than you might think, especially if you have been used to using titles like

'Noughts and Crosses by Malorie Blackman'

or

'Travel Brochures'

Your title should be short and to the point but it should give a hint of what your writing is going to be about.

It is always better to make your title specific – to show the reader that you have a clear focus for your essay. So, if your intention is to write about the dialect used in a particular part of Scotland, use a title like this:

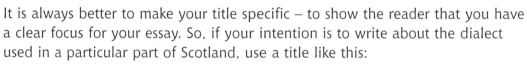
'An Analysis of the Dialect spoken in West Aberdeenshire and the Reasons for its Use'

Instead of

'West Aberdeenshire Dialect'

'The Language of Advertising – how adverts persuade us to buy'

is a more effective title than

'Adverts'

Two-minute Task

Read the titles below – which do you think is the most effective and why? Which do you think is the least effective and why?

The theme of love in 'The Cone Gatherers' by Robin Jenkins

'Mid Term Break' by Seamus Heaney

The language of the 'Sun' newspaper

'Shrek' – is Shrek a traditional fairy tale hero?

A comparison of two films by Martin Scorcese

Football commentating and why it is important

Proposal

So you have chosen your title and it is perfect – what do you do next? You have to make clear what your intention (sometimes called a proposal) is at the start of your writing. 'At the start' means in the first paragraph.

Is your intention to

- analyse a character
- compare two short stories
- write about a film
- write about an aspect of language
- write about an aspect of media, for example, advertising?

Your intention should not only explain what you are going to write about. It should also explain how you are going to write the essay. This is the start of structuring or organising your essay.

I am going to write about Susie in 'The Lovely Bones' by Alice Sebold. Susie is the dead narrator of the novel and the main character. She tells the story from 'heaven'. I will write an analysis of Susie, concentrating in the first half of my essay on her life and relationships and in the second half of my essay, I will write about 'heaven' and whether Susie is happy there.

Pair and Share

Read over this first paragraph or 'proposal' with a partner. Are the statements below true or false? Talk this over with a partner and agree on your decision.

The main character of the novel is Susie.   true/false

The writer of this Personal Study is Alice Sebold.   true/false

The Personal Study will be in five sections.   true/false

This proposal sounds interesting.   true/false

A good title would be *Susie*   true/false

Quick Think

What is your proposal/intention? Start off your answer with 'I am going to write about … '

Organising your writing

Organisation is vital. Your writing **must** 'do what it says on the tin'! Or rather 'do what it says in the title'!

Your essay must be clearly **organised** and **expressed**, whether you are writing about a text(s) or a topic(s). This means it must have a clear **beginning**, **middle** and **end**. An **introduction** (first paragraph) and **conclusion** (last paragraph) are essential. Both should state clearly your focus and intention. Think of them as the bread in a sandwich – if you don't use bread at the top and the bottom, the middle of the sandwich will fall out!

Your **proposal** will form the **first paragraph** of your essay. Let's move on to the '**main body**' of the writing – the filling in the middle of the sandwich!

top bread = introduction

filling = main body

bottom bread = conclusion

How to write about a text

This section is about the main body of a Personal Study (PS) text. If you have chosen to write about a topic(s), move on to page 81.

(Refer back to the section about Critical Essay writing in the **'Reading'** chapter for lots of useful advice about writing for a text.)

Many Intermediate 1 candidates write about novels they have enjoyed reading, so we will use a novel – *Eagle Strike* by Anthony Horowitz – for our example here. Again, check with your teacher for advice on writing about other types of text.

Focus

You will probably be used to writing 'Book Reports'. If so, then you will know that you would include in your book report all the aspects listed below, writing a short section on each. Now is the time, however, to concentrate on only **one** (or perhaps **two)** of these aspects. This is called your **'focus'**.

- characterisation
- plot
- theme
- language
- setting

(If you don't get it at first, think of taking a picture with a camera. There may be lots of detail in the background but you focus on a person's face or the most colourful flower.)

Mind map

Whichever 'focus' you choose, mind mapping is a useful way of planning what you are going to write. (If mind mapping is not 'your thing', you can make notes in another way if you prefer. The important thing is to **make notes** before you start writing – the way you do this is up to you.)

Let's imagine you have chosen to write about the main character in *Eagle Strike*. A mind map is done for you here.

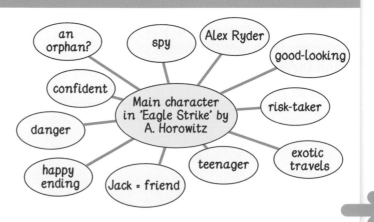

Pair and Share

Looking at the mind map, and even if you have not read this book, can you suggest an **order** for these ideas? Number each idea so if you think 'risk-taker' would be the first thing you would write about, make this number 1, and so on …

Talk this over with a partner and agree on your decision.

Organisation

Your teacher will help you with how to **organise** your writing (always bearing in mind that you only have **one** hour to write the final draft of your essay). It goes without saying that you must use paragraphs and that these must be in a logical order. All the ideas you include must be relevant to your focus.

There is a lot more to it than that, though. When writing about a text(s), you must show that:

- you have understood the main points of the text(s) by referring to relevant features of the text
- you can analyse some of the main features of the text(s) and how they add to the effect of the text
- you have a personal reaction to the text(s), using evidence
- you can express yourself clearly, making your focus easy to follow
- you are mainly accurate in your spelling, grammar and punctuation.

What is meant by 'main features'?

In a **novel or short story**, the main features are:

- characterisation
- language
- plot
- setting
- theme

In a **poem**, the main features are:

- content
- language
- shape or pattern
- theme

In a **play**, the main features are:

- characterisation
- language
- plot
- setting
- theme

If there is another feature you would like to write about, discuss this with your teacher. There are thousands of texts to choose from for your Personal Study and there is not enough space to include them all here … and each one is original and different. You are spoiled for choice!

'Using evidence'

Golden Rule number 1: you must remember to include quotations when you are writing about a text at Intermediate 1 level, or at any other level, for that matter – it is an important part of any writing about literature.

If you make a point about an aspect of a text – say, that the writer has created a gloomy and mysterious atmosphere – you must use evidence from the text to prove or 'back up' your idea. If you use a direct quote, always make sure you have copied it exactly. You can also use your own words to explain what the author has written. A mixture of evidence using direct quotes and your own words is best.

Never forget that your evidence must be **relevant** – in other words, do not use a quotation just because you like it! If you are writing about setting, do not use a quotation about a character or about a theme or anything else.

Quick Think

Look at the two statements below – which quotation is more relevant?

The writer has created a gloomy and mysterious atmosphere within the haunted castle: 'Lord Rochester sneered at the young girl crying at his feet'.

'A dense fog and cold silence surrounded the castle': the writer has created a gloomy and mysterious atmosphere within the haunted castle.

Did you notice that the quotations above are introduced or finished with a semi-colon and that the quotation is part of the sentence? This is the best way to write your quotations. The examiner will be underwhelmed if you write the following:

The writer has created a gloomy and mysterious atmosphere within the haunted castle. It says 'A dense fog and cold silence surrounded the castle.'

'Personal reaction'

Your 'personal reaction' to the text is the way that you 'connect' with the text. If you really love (or really hate!) a book or story, this will be very obvious in your essay – mostly through the words and ideas you use. The way to show your 'personal reaction' to a text is to write your opinions clearly and use words like 'I' and 'my' to show that you have personal thoughts and feelings about the text – about the way the author writes, about the characters, plot, ending – everything!

You may be used to doing this at the end of an essay in the conclusion where you recommend a book or say what you thought of it. At Intermediate 1 level, you can add this in a 'block' but ideally your 'personal reaction' should be scattered throughout your whole essay.

Quick Think

If you are thinking of writing about a text(s), which writer might you choose? Do you feel you have a 'personal engagement' with the texts of this writer? If so, why?

Do you remember reading about 'Evaluation' in the **'Reading'** chapter? Here is a reminder:

To answer questions marked 'E' for Evaluation, you must express your opinions about the passage! Evaluation questions ask you to comment on the ideas and words in the passage. They often ask, for example, how effective an idea or image or word is.

In your Personal Study, always include your comments and opinions on how effective the writer has been – this is your 'personal reaction'.

Two top tips

Finally, two top tips. **First**, you must always write about literature in the **present tense**. This is a simple rule and you must stick to it, even if a book has been written in the past tense. Remember – always comment on the content in the present tense.

Secondly, always remember that the characters in a novel or play are **not real** people – they have been created by a writer! You must show that you realise this when you write about any text.

Pair and Share

Look at these statements about the main character in the film *Forrest Gump*.

1. Forrest Gump is a lonely man who finds it difficult to find and keep a job.
2. The writer describes Forrest Gump as a lonely character who finds it difficult to find and keep a job.

What is the difference between statement 1 and statement 2?

Talk this over with your partner and agree on your decision.

How to write about a topic

You may decide to write about a **topic** rather than a text for your Personal Study. This is usually an aspect of language, for example, the language of advertising or newspapers or an aspect of spoken language.

Remember that this unit is all about independent study. You must carry out research on your topic and your teacher will help you with where to look. There is advice on researching in the 'Basic skills' section of the **'Reading'** chapter on page 12.

Once you have chosen your topic, do as much reading and research as you can about it. Use the internet, books, newpapers and so on. Your teacher will let you know how much time you have to do this.

Focus

Choose the main aspect you want to write about. This is called your '**focus**'. (If you don't get it at first, think of taking a picture with a camera. There may be lots of detail in the background but you focus on a person's face or the most colourful flower.)

Mind map

Whichever 'focus' you choose, mind mapping is a useful way of planning what you are going to write. (If mind mapping is not your thing, you can make notes in another way if you prefer. The important thing is to **make notes** before you start writing – the way you do this is up to you.)

Let's imagine you have chosen to write about the language of newspapers – a comparison of the *Sun* and *The Times*, for example. A mind map is done for you here of the language of the *Sun*.

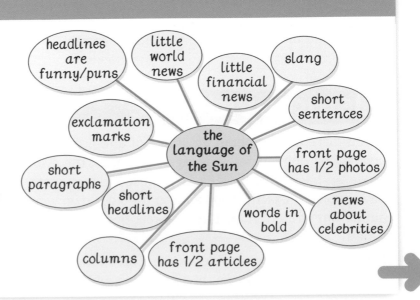

Pair and Share

Looking at the mind map, can you suggest whether some of these ideas might 'go together' to form different sections in your essay?

Make a list of ideas that might 'go together' to form sections. For example, one section might be 'Headlines'.

Talk this over with your partner and agree on your decision.

Organisation

Your teacher will help you with how to **organise** your writing (always bearing in mind that you only have **one** hour to write the final draft of your essay). It goes without saying that you must use paragraphs and that these must be in a logical order. All the ideas you include must be relevant to your focus.

There is a lot more to it than that, though. When writing about a topic(s), you must show that:

- you have understood the main points of the topic(s), by referring to relevant features of the topic(s)
- you can analyse some of the main features of the topic(s), and how they add to the effect of the topic(s)
- you have a personal reaction to the topic(s), using evidence
- you can express yourself clearly, making your focus easy to follow
- you are mainly accurate in your spelling, grammar and punctuation.

What is meant by 'main features'?

The main features in any type of topic are usually

- audience
- purpose
- content
- style
- layout/format
- structure

If there is another feature you want to write about, discuss this with your teacher. There are thousands of topics to choose from for your Personal Study and there is not enough space to include them all here ... and each one is original and different. You are spoiled for choice!

'Using evidence'

If you make a point about an aspect of a topic – say, that the writer has used very strong opinionated language – you must use evidence from the text to prove or 'back up' your idea. If you use a direct quote, always make sure you have copied it exactly. You can also use your own words to explain what the author has written. A mixture of direct quotes and evidence in your own words is best.

Never forget that your evidence must be relevant – in other words, do not use a quotation just because you like it!

Quick Think

Look at the statement below – which quotation is more relevant?

> The writer uses very strong, opinionated language against racism: 'I hate the way the Scots degrade and de-humanise these fine people'.

Or

> 'There are over one million immigrants living and working in Scotland today': the writer uses very strong, opinionated language against racism.

Did you notice that the quotations above are introduced or finished with a semi-colon and that the quotation is part of the sentence? This is the best way to write your quotations. The examiner will be underwhelmed if you write the following:

> The writer uses very strong opinionated language against racism. It says 'I hate the way the Scots degrade and de-humanise these fine people'.

'Personal reaction'

The way to show your 'personal reaction' to a topic is to write your opinions clearly and use words like 'I' and 'my' to show that you have personal thoughts and feelings about the topic.

Ideally your 'personal reaction' should be scattered throughout your whole essay.

Do you remember reading about 'Evaluation' in the **'Reading'** chapter? Here is a reminder!

Quick Think

If you are thinking of writing about a topic(s), which topic would you choose? Do you feel that you have a 'personal reaction' to texts about this topic?

To answer questions marked 'E' for Evaluation, you must express your opinions about the passage! Evaluation questions ask you to comment on the ideas and words in the passage. They often ask, for example, how effective an idea or image or word is.

In your Personal Study, always include your comments and opinions on how effective the writer has been – this is your 'personal reaction'.

Two top tips

Finally, two top tips. **First**, you must always write about a topic in the **present tense**. It's a simple rule, but you **must** stick to it!

Secondly, do not fall into the trap of **writing about the topic itself** – this can happen if you are writing about a topic such as homelessness, for example.

Conclusion

It is amazing how much time students spend on making the introduction to a piece of writing perfect – and completely forget about the conclusion! Remember – you have only **one** hour to write your final draft and if time runs out, it is the conclusion which is often left out. Even if you have not covered all the points you want to make in the main body of your essay, always try to 'finish off' a piece of writing.

- Your conclusion should always mention your focus again.
- Remind the reader of what your intention (or 'proposal') was and explain whether you feel you have achieved this.
- Summarise the main points of your essay in a general statement at the end.
- You can include a quotation – but only if it is relevant and you have not used it earlier!

In your final assessment, you are allowed to refer to materials such as your text, your outline and any notes you have made (no more than two pages).

Good luck – and enjoy writing!

Target Time

Time to set **your** targets for your **written** Personal Study. Refer back to pages 9 and 10 for more information on target setting.

My target is to achieve Grade .... in my Personal Study because

....

....

....

To achieve this grade, I am going to work on

....

....

....

What's it all about?

You have the choice to do a **spoken** presentation on your text or topic. This must be discussed with your teacher.

This chapter is quite short as much of the advice has already been given in the first section – about the choice of your **text/topic**, **organisation**, **focus** and **content** of the piece. The one main difference is that you will **'speak'** your presentation rather than writing an essay.

- Your presentation must last for a minimum of **three** minutes.
- You will be asked questions following your presentation – at least **three** questions are likely. These will ask you to expand on points made earlier in your presentation.
- There must be **three** or more people in your audience.

Choice of text or topic

Your teacher will advise you about your choice of text or topic and about exactly what is expected of you in your final assessment. Your teacher will expect you to:

- use appropriate vocabulary and tone in your presentation
- use a variety of sentence structures in your presentation
- be appropriate to your purpose and audience
- vary the pace of your presentation
- use appropriate eye contact, posture and gesture.

Performance Criteria

When speaking about a topic(s), you must show that:

- you have understood the main points of the topic(s), by referring to relevant features of the topic(s)
- you can analyse some of the main features of the topic(s) and how they add to the effect of the topic(s)
- you have a personal reaction to the topic(s), using evidence
- you can express yourself audibly and use verbal and non-verbal techniques, making your focus easy to follow
- you can interact with your audience and be aware of them, providing relevant answers to their questions.

Let's look at some of the phrases within these Performance Criteria in more detail.

'Audibly'

Make sure your audience can hear what you are saying! Practice makes perfect and the more you can talk – in front of friends, family, the mirror – the better. Speak to your teacher about using microphones or other equipment which may help.

'Verbal and non-verbal techniques'

Make use of your voice … don't just speak in one tone! Inject some enthusiasm into your voice and you will find your audience will be much more interested in what you have to say. 'Non-verbal techniques' are techniques such as body language and hand gestures. Although these things may not seem important, they add up and create an impression. Think about whether you will stand or sit to deliver your talk. What will you do with your hands (remember that nervous gestures may distract your listeners)? Do you fidget when you are nervous? Work on ways to cut down any distractions for your audience.

'You must interact with your audience and be aware of them, providing relevant answers to their questions'

While you are giving your talk, use your eyes to look around. Make contact with your listeners by smiling, nodding, looking at them …

Be ready for any questions at the end by thinking beforehand about what your listeners might ask. Prepare answers to a few questions so you are ready.

Reference materials

In your final assessment, you are allowed to refer to materials such as your text, your outline and any notes you have made (no more than two pages).

Your teacher may record your talk or use a checklist. These must both be kept along with any notes or materials you use on the day.

You must take great care **not** to read out a previously prepared essay or script – this assessment is about talking, not about writing! You should refer to notes only. Also be very careful that you do not learn a script off by heart and 'recite' it. Again, this is not a spontaneous spoken presentation. Ask your teacher for advice if you are unsure about this.

Target Time

Time to set **your** targets for your **spoken** Personal Study. Refer back to pages 9 and 10 for more information on target setting.

My target is to achieve Grade .... in my Personal Study because

....

....

....

To achieve this grade, I am going to work on

....

....

....

Internal and external assessment

The **'Intermediate 1 English Course and what it involves'** section at the beginning of the book explained which assessments are internal and which are external. Look back to remind yourself of the course requirements.

The table of internal/external assessments is copied again for you below.

Internal Assessments	Close Reading Writing Textual Analysis
External Assessments	Close Reading (45 minutes) Critical Essay (45 minutes)

You must pass the **three internal** parts of the course as well as pass **both** the **external** assessments to gain an overall pass.

The external exam will last for **1 hour and 30 minutes**. There will be two papers as follows:

Close Reading (45 minutes)

You will have to show that you can understand, analyse and evaluate a prose passage by answering questions on the passage.

Critical Essay (45 minutes)

You will choose **one** question from a number of questions and write an essay in answer to the question. You will write about a text you have studied as part of the course. This can be poetry, prose, drama, media or a language text.

There is usually a break of 20 minutes between the papers. Close Reading is usually first, followed by the Critical Essay.

Exam skills

This section will help you to survive your external exam – and who knows – you might even enjoy it!

Close Reading paper

Let's look first of all at the Close Reading paper.

The best way to prepare for the examination is to practise, practise, then practise some more! You should read as much as you can – quality newspapers, novels, non-fiction texts, etc. The more you read, the more practised you will become and the more vocabulary you will know. Get into the habit of keeping a dictionary beside you so that you can check out words you do not know. Even better, keep a 'vocabulary jotter' beside you so you can keep a note of these words and their meanings.

The more passages you read and the more questions you answer will help you to work out exactly what to expect. Remember that the questions will always be marked with **U, A** or **E**.

Quick Think

Can you remember (without looking back) what **U, A** and **E** mean? Can you recall what each type of question will ask you?

Practice makes perfect ...

In the actual exam, you will have to manage your time well. It is very important not only to **practise** the skills you will need (**reading** and **answering**) but also to practise **using these skills within 45 minutes**. You will have to practise two or three times **at least** to know how long you usually take to complete the answers on a passage. Perhaps you are writing too much for each question? Or, if you finish very quickly, perhaps you are not writing enough?

Look at a suggested 'time plan' below.

	Total 45 minutes
Read the introduction, read through the passage.	5 minutes
Read the passage again.	5 minutes
Answer the questions.	30 minutes
Read over your answers.	5 minutes

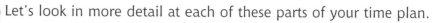
Let's look in more detail at each of these parts of your time plan.

Read the introduction, read through the passage
(approximately 5 minutes)

Never ignore the introduction – it gives you valuable information about the passage and will help you in understanding the purpose of the text (look back for more information about **'purpose'** in the **'Reading'** chapter of the book). You also should think about the **title** of the passage, if there is one – there is sometimes a question about the title, so be sure you understand it before you start reading.

Look at the introduction and opening to the 2003 Close Reading paper.

> **The passage which follows is adapted from the book 'Down Under' in which Bill Bryson describes his experiences in Australia.**
>
> *Boogie-Boarding*
>
> *'Excuse me for interrupting,' I interrupted, 'but what is boogie-boarding exactly?'*
>
> *'Oh, it's fun'…*

You can tell a lot from these few lines! The passage has been 'adapted' from the original book which means the passage has had some words and phrases changed or added or missed out. You know already that the book is about Australia and that it is written in the first person – Bill Bryson is writing a first-hand account of what happened to him in Australia. Boogie-boarding is a fun, sporty activity for young people so you could guess that the passage might be light-hearted and, in fact, the passage has some humour in it – for example, the repetition of 'interrupting/interrupted'.

Read the passage again (approximately 5 minutes)

Don't forget the advice in the **'Reading'** chapter to re-read the passage. Many candidates move straight on to the questions but it is much better to have a real understanding of the passage first. You will find the questions easier if you do!

Answer the questions (approximately 30 minutes)

This part is what will take up most of your time. Try not to rush and pay attention to the marks allocated to each question – this will help you to work out how much to write.

Get to know the wording of the questions. Make sure you understand what the following words mean:

Give evidence	quote
Explain in your own words	do not quote
Identify	find (and explain)
Convey	to put across to the reader
By close reference	read the words very carefully
Comment	explain

→ Read over your answers (approximately 5 minutes)

Always leave time to read over your answers. They must make sense and have accurate spelling and punctuation. You may have the correct answer but if the examiner cannot work out what you mean, you may lose marks!

Pair and Share

What are the time management issues for you when answering questions on passages? Do you run out of time?

Talk this over with a partner and agree on how you can both improve your time management.

Critical Essay

Now for the Critical Essay.

You have 45 minutes for the Critical Essay. You will be given several questions – there are usually **two** questions for **Drama**, **two** for **Prose**, **two** for **Poetry**, **two** for **Mass Media** and **two** for **Language**. Remember that you will write only **one** essay.

You will probably already have decided what genre you are going to write about. If so, read the two questions and decide which 'fits' best for your text. If you have prepared more than one genre, read over the other questions. There is nothing worse than starting to write an essay and then deciding it is the wrong one for you! This will lose you valuable time. So take your time to pick the right question.

Quick Think

Look at the two prose questions from 2004.

Choose a novel or a short story which has an important turning point that changes things for one of the characters.

Show how the story builds up to the turning point and say why it is important for the character.

In your answer you should refer to such features as: structure, character, or any other appropriate feature.

OR

Choose a novel or a short story or a piece of non-fiction or a group of prose texts which deal with a topic of importance to society.

Say what you learned about the topic from your reading and whether you felt sympathy for the people involved.

In your answer you should refer to such features as: theme, character, or any other appropriate feature.

Which question would you choose if you had prepared a prose text?

Once you have chosen your question, take some time to highlight the key words and phrases in the question.

Pair and Share

Choose one of the questions from the previous page and highlight the key words and phrases on your own. Your partner should do the same.

Now compare your highlighted words. Did you choose the same ones?

Choosing and highlighting your question should take about five minutes. Now start writing, using all the advice in the 'Reading' chapter about writing an introduction, main body and conclusion.

At all times, remember to answer the question – don't just write everything you know about a text. You are being examined on your ability to answer the question!

Always leave time at the end – perhaps five minutes – to read over your essay. Check the spelling and punctuation – take care to check whether you have set out and punctuated your quotations correctly. Check that each sentence makes sense and that you have a conclusion (even if you have run out of time, try to add a final sentence referring to the question).

In all your timed assessments, try to write neatly and legibly! If the examiner or your teacher cannot read your writing, they cannot confidently award you any marks!

And finally, the very best of luck!

Target Time

Just before your exam, it is useful to remind yourself of what you have to do to gain an A, B or a C. Read over the **performance criteria** again to focus on what you have to do – these are explained in the **'Reading'** chapter.

Time to set **your** targets for your exams in **Close Reading** and **Critical Essay** Refer back to page 10 for more information on target setting.

My target is to achieve Grade .... in my Close Reading and Critical Essay exam because

....

....

....

To achieve this grade, I am going to work on

....

....

....

Index